DISSENTING ACADEMIES IN ENGLAND

Their Rise and Progress and their Place among the Educational Systems of the Country

by

IRENE PARKER

1969

OCTAGON BOOKS

New York

First published 1914

Reprinted 1969
by permission of the Cambridge University Press

OCTAGON BOOKS
A DIVISION OF FARRAR, STRAUS & GIROUX, INC.
19 Union Square West
New York, N. Y. 10003

LIBRARY OF CONGRESS CATALOG CARD NUMBER: 70-96189

Printed in U.S.A. by
TAYLOR PUBLISHING COMPANY
DALLAS, TEXAS

TO

MY FATHER

TO WHOM I OWE MY INTEREST
BOTH IN NONCONFORMITY AND EDUCATION

PREFACE

IT is difficult to understand why the contribution made to Education by Puritanism and Dissent has not yet been fully investigated. The subject is a vast one and it was with the hope of touching upon the fringe of it that a few years ago I devoted my leisure time to making an inquiry into the part played by the Dissenting Academies. No one can realize more clearly than I how totally inadequate is the account here given; if it serve to show that there exists a field worthy of research the labour will be amply repaid.

I should like to acknowledge my indebtedness to Sir Alfred Dale and Professor Campagnac for valuable help and encouragement in my work, and to Dr Selbie for kindness in seeing it through the press.

IRENE PARKER.

OXFORD, 1914.

CONTENTS

PART I

PART II

PART III

SOURCES

The following are the most important books which have been consulted.

ABBEY and OVERTON. *The English Church in the Eighteenth Century.*

AIKEN, JOHN. *Life of.*

BOGUE and BENNETT. *History of Dissenters.*

BROWN, E. E. *Monograph on Secondary Education in U.S.A.*

CALAMY. *Account of Silenced Ministers.*
— *Continuation of the Account.*
— *History of his own Life and Times.*
— *Abridgement of Baxter's Life.*

Cambridge Modern History, vols. i, ii, vi.

Castle Hill Church, Northampton, History of.

CLARK. *Life and Times of Antony Wood.*
— *Reminiscences of Oxford.*

CLEGG, JAMES. *Diary of.*
— *Life of Rev. John Ashe.*

COWLEY, A. *Proposition for the Advancement of Experimental Philosophy.*

DALE, R. W. *History of Congregationalism in England.*

DAVIES. *The Tewkesbury Academy with sketches of its Tutor and Students.*

DE MONTMORENCY. *The Progress of Education in England.*
— *State Intervention in Education.*

DEFOE. *Earlier Life and chief Early Works of.* Ed. H. MORLEY.

DIRCKS. *Biographical Memoir of S. Hartlib.*

Documents relating to the Act of Uniformity.

DURY, J. *The Reformed School.*

GIBBON. *Memoirs of my Life and Writings.*

GIBBONS, THOS. *Memoirs of the Rev. Isaac Watts.*

GORDON. *Early Nonconformity and Education.*

GRAVES. *Peter Ramus.*

GREEN, J. R. *Studies in Oxford History chiefly in the Eighteenth Century.*

GROVE, H. *Works of.*

HALL, JOHN. *An Humble motion to the Parliament of England concerning the advancement of learning.*

HALLEY. *Lancashire Puritanism and Nonconformity.*

HARTLIB, S. *True and Readie Way to learne the Latin Tongue.*
— *Considerations leading to the Happy Accomplishment of England's Reformation in Church and State.*

HENRY, M. *Life of P. Henry.*

HESTER, GILES. *Attercliffe as a Seat of Learning.*

HEYWOOD, OLIVER. *Autobiography and Diaries of.*

HOW, S. *Sufficiency of Spirit's Teaching without Humane learning.*

HULL. *Economic Writings of Sir W. Petty.*

HUMPHREYS. *Correspondence and diary of P. Doddridge.*

HUNTER, JOSEPH. *The Rise of the old Dissent as exemplified in the life of Oliver Heywood.*

HURDIE. *Vindication of Magdalen College from the Aspersions of Mr Gibbon.*

HUXLEY. *Essay on Joseph Priestley.*

LEACH, A. F. *History of Winchester College.*
— *Grammar Schools at Reformation.*
— *Educational Charters and Documents.*

McDONNELL. *History of St Paul's School.*

MAGRATH. *The Flemings in Oxford.*

MANN, H. *Education in Great Britain.*

Manuscript Accounts of Ministers (Dr Williams's Library).

MASSON. *Life of Milton.*

Monthly Repository—especially vols. iv, v, viii, xi.

MULLINGER. *The University of Cambridge.*

NEWCOME, H. *Diary and Autobiography of.*

NEWTH. *Senatus Academicus* (Associated Theological Colleges).

NIGHTINGALE. *Non-conformity in Lancashire.*

ORTON. *Memoirs of the Life, Character and Writings of Rev. P. Doddridge.*

PEACHAM. *Compleat Gentleman.*

PETTY. *Advice of W. P. to Mr S. H. for the advancement of learning.*

POOLE, MAT. *Model for the maintaining of students of choice abilities at the Universities.*

PRIESTLEY. *Miscellaneous Works* (Essay on Education).

— *Rudiments of English Grammar.*

Proceedings at the Opening of Manchester College, Oxford.

RAIT. *Life in the Medieval University.*

RUTT. *Life and Correspondence of Joseph Priestley.*

STOUGHTON. *Ph. Doddridge, his life and labours.*

— *Religion under Queen Anne and the Georges.*

TOULMIN. *Historical view of the State of Protestant Dissenters in England.*

Transactions of the Historical Society of Lancashire and Cheshire.

Transactions of the Congregational Historical Society.

TURNER. *Lives of Eminent Unitarians.*

Victoria County Histories.

WAKEFIELD, GILBERT. *Autobiography of.*

WATSON. *The Beginnings of the Teaching of Modern Subjects in England.*

WARD, SETH. *Vindiciae Academiarum.*

WEBSTER. *Examination of Academies.*

Wesley-Palmer Controversy Letters.

WILSON, WALTER. *History and Antiquities of Dissenting Churches and meeting houses, London, Westminster and Southwark.*

WOOD, ANTONY. *History and Antiquities of the Colleges and Halls in the University of Oxford.*

WOODWARD, H. *A Light to Grammar.*

— *Gate to the Sciences.*

I

THE DEVELOPMENT OF REALISM IN ENGLAND

The development of educational opinion has been so remarkable during the last century that it is generally held that all our modern educational ideas had their birth after 1800. No greater mistake can be made. The fundamental principles of modern English education were in process of formation during the two preceding centuries. The period covered by the years 1600–1800 is the one in which the education of the middle classes in ' modern ' subjects was first not merely advocated but attempted. It was advocated chiefly by the Puritans in the first half of the 17th century ; it was attempted by the Tutors of the Dissenting Academies. Before describing the work of these Academies it is necessary to trace the rise of the educational principles to which they gave expression.

At the beginning of the 17th century our three great educational systems, the University, the Grammar School and the Elementary School were all in existence. The elementary school, represented by the old song, writing, and cyphering schools (which cannot here be dealt with) gave boys the education required on their entrance to secondary education in the grammar schools. The universities and grammar schools are both very ancient systems ; the former date back to the 12th century ; the latter to the coming of Christian missionaries to the English.

The grammar or language schools (*ludus literarius*) have their origin in the Cathedral schools founded quite early in the history of the Church in this country. Augustine and his fellow missionaries were not long in finding that preaching had to be supplemented by teaching ; converts had to be trained to help in the Christianization of the whole country and to take part in the services of the Church. Very soon after the establishment of Churches therefore, schools, modelled on those of Rome in which the missionaries themselves had been educated and where they had probably taught, were started often in some part of the Church building itself and later, when our Cathedrals were built, schools attached to them were built also. The earliest record of the establishment of such a school is as follows : ' At this time (631)...After his (Sigebert, King of the East Angles) return home, as soon as he obtained the throne, wishing to imitate what he had seen well ordered among the Gauls, he set up a school in which boys might be taught grammar. He was assisted therein by Bishop Felix, who came to him from Kent, and provided them with pedagogues and masters after the fashion of the Canterbury men[1].' This of course indicates that a grammar school had been already established in Canterbury. It will be remembered that Alcuin, the schoolmaster of York, was persuaded to leave England to teach in the schools founded by Charlemagne.

From the first, then, education was regarded as a

[1] A. F. Leach, *Educational Charters*, p. 3.

branch of Church work ; ' the school was an adjunct of the Church.' The close connection thus established had a profound and far-reaching effect ; it at once determined control and curriculum. At the head of a Cathedral school was a cleric, the greater part of whose time was given to teaching. Both as cleric and school-master he was subject to his bishop who consequently exercised a very definite control over the school. So natural and even necessary did this Church control seem that later, when schools were founded by the Guilds or hospitals or by private people, the founders invariably placed them under ecclesiastical supervision[1].

The curriculum also was influenced by this con-nection with the Church. The Catholic schools were founded to train clergymen and they had therefore to teach Latin, which was not merely the language of the Church, but the one language of educated Christendom. Latin, therefore, was not merely *a* subject, it was *the* subject—it was, in fact, the whole curriculum. The language or grammar schools were the only schools which during the Middle Ages provided a classical education—a definite distinction must be made be-tween them and the monastery schools which came into being later. The two were alike in so far as they both trained youths for a definite career ; but while the grammar schools trained boys who were to be

---

[1] ' For close on 1100 years, from 598–1670, all educational institutions were under exclusively ecclesiastical control. The law of education was a branch of the Canon law. The Church courts had exclusive jurisdiction over schools and universities and colleges and until 1580 all schoolmasters and scholars were clerks, or clerics, or clergy, and in orders, though not necessarily holy orders,' A. F. Leach, *Educational Charters*, Introd. p. xii.

clergymen and who were therefore taught Latin, the
monastery schools trained novices or oblates who were
to be monks and who were therefore taught singing,
writing, illuminating ; the prayers of the Church ; the
rules of their order.   The monastery schools rarely com-
peted with the Cathedral grammar schools in the provision of a classical education.

The boys who attended the grammar schools were
the younger (poor) sons of the squires and the sons of
yeomen farmers.   The sons of the nobles and their
pages (the eldest sons of the squires) had tutors at
home.   After the rise of the wealthy middle class, it
was their boys who filled the town grammar schools
such as St Paul's and it then became customary for
the gentry to send their sons to boarding grammar
schools such as Eton, Westminster and Shrewsbury.
On entering a grammar school a boy was expected to
have received a fair grounding in accidence (or a knowledge of the concords at least) and to possess ability
to speak and write correctly in English—these foundations were laid in the song or writing schools or at home.
The boy was then guided through the remainder of
the accidence and afterwards proceeded to the reading
of a few Latin authors ; to the formation of a good
style in prose and verse and to the acquisition of the
ease and elegance of a Cicero in disputations.   The
scarcity and, so far as the scholars were concerned,
the total absence of books made the class work very
laborious.   The method (and the uniformity which is
seen in control and curriculum is found in the method
lso) was as follows.   First, the text was dictated to
the boys, then punctuated and read through, then

construed and finally translated so that considerable time must have been spent in reading one book. Occasionally an enthusiastic teacher commented on the subject matter ; but for the majority it was enough to get through the reading and translation only. In such comments and explanations as were given was contained all the instruction in ' natural history,' history or geography which the boys received. Once a week a repetition of the week's work was required. Verse writing was an important part of the work in the upper classes and disputes were held sometimes as often as three times a week, while public disputations in the presence of the clergy were always held on feast days. The Eton time-table of 1530 shows exactly what was done in practically all the grammar schools during the 15th and 16th centuries.

But it is with education in the 17th century particularly that this book attempts to deal. The grammar school of the 17th century was in almost every detail identical with that of the preceding centuries. Compare with the Eton time-table of 1530 the one at St Paul's almost 150 years later. From 1672–1697 the head of St Paul's was Thos. Gale and among his MSS. in the Library of Trinity College, Cambridge, is one entitled ' The Constant Method of Teaching in St Paul's, London.' This is really the time-table for each of the eight forms ; it may be tabulated as follows :

ETON TIME-TABLE, 1530.

From *Educational Charters*, A. F. Leach, p. 451.

	Mondaye.	Tewysdaye.	Wedenysdaye.	Thursdaye.	Frydaye.	Saterdaye.
The Fyrst Forme.	Parte of stanbridge accidence every mornyng with the second, thrid, and fowrth forme. Institutiones parvulorum Vocabula. And also Latynes.	Idem	Idem	Idem	Quos decet in mensa at after-none renderyng Rules.	Quos decet in mensa at the afternone render Latynys.
The Seconde Forme	ffabulae Aesopi, Genera Lilii Latynys 4 tymys in the weke.	Idem	Idem	Idem	Cato at the after none rulys.	Cato and at the afternone render Latynys and Vulgares.
The Thrid Forme.	Terence Preterita Lilii. Latynys.	Idem	Idem	Idem	Most proper Hymmys. at the after none render rulys.	Properest hymmys. afternone render Latynys and Vulgars.

The Fourthe Forme.	Terentius, Octo Partes Lilii Latyns twies every weke.	Idem	Idem	Idem	Vergilii buccolica in the mornyng. At the after none render rulys.	Vergilii buccolica at afternone render the Latynys and Vulgars.
The Fyfthe Forme.	Wrytyng of a theme, Versi-fyeng rulys drawne owte of despauterius and other modus conscribendi epistolas.	The same save they make verses.	The same save they make nothyng.	Epistole tullii makyng of epistles beside Salustius.	Vergilii Eneis in mornyng at after none renderyng of rul(y)s lernyd the hole weke.	Vergilii Eneis repetyng of latyns and vulgars lernyd that weke.
The Syxte fforme and the Seventhe Form.	Horatius or tullius mosellanys figures or Copia rerum et verborum of Erasmus.	All lyke Monday save they make verses.	Like as afore save they make nothyng.	Epistole Tullii making of Eplis beside Horatius.	Vergilii Eneis in mornyng at after none renderyng of rul(y)s lernid the hole weke.	Vergilii Eneis repetyng of latyns and vulgars lernyd all ye weke.

Every Quarter one fortenyght every forme rendryth all thyngs lernyd that quarter.

TIME-TABLE OF ST PAUL'S GRAMMAR SCHOOL, c. 1690[1].

Class		Monday.	Tuesday.	Wednesday.	Thursday.	Friday.	Saturday.
1–4.		Latin Gram.	Latin Gram.	Latin Gram.	Latin Gram.	Repetition of week's work.	Latin Gram.

In the *afternoon* Ovid's *Metamorphosis* read in 4th class and the *Tristia* in the 3rd.

Class		Monday.	Tuesday.	Wednesday.	Thursday.	Friday.	Saturday.
5.	*Morn.*	Latin Gram.	Greek Gram.	Latin Gram.	Greek Gram.	Latin Gram.	Greek Gram.
	Aft.	Psalms into Lat. Verse.	Vergil.	Psalms to Lat. Verse.	Martial.	Psalms to Lat. Verse.	Sallust.
6.	*Morn.*	Greek Gram.	Greek Gram.	Greek Gram.	Greek Gram.	Greek Gram.	Greek Gram.
	Aft.	Moral theme.	Greek Test.	Moral theme.	Martial, Vergil.	Moral theme.	Divine theme.
7.	*Morn.*	Minor poets.	Greek Gram.	Minor poets.	Greek Gram.	Minor poets.	Greek Gram.
	Aft.	Moral theme.	Horace, Apollodorus.	Theme.	Cicero Oratione.	Theme.	Theme.
8.	*Morn.*	Heb. Psalter or Gram.	Hebrew.	Hebrew.	Hebrew.	Hebrew.	Hebrew.
	Aft.	Moral theme.	Homer, Demosthenes.	Moral theme.	Persius, Juvenal.	Theme.	Divine theme.

" themes of the upper forms seem to have been set as 'home work'"—to be done in the afternoons—probably Wednesday afternoon should be shown as a holiday.

[1] This time-table is drawn up from material given in *The History of St Paul's School*, McDonnell, p. 265 *et seq.*

Lists of books[1] and time-tables of other schools might be given to illustrate the fact that century after century both as regards curriculum and method the grammar schools remained substantially unaltered. That is to say, they continued to confine their attention to the trivium—grammar, rhetoric and logic; Latin, a little Greek and, in some cases, a little Hebrew—these were the only subjects ; verse-writing, themes and disputations the only exercises. After passing through seven or eight forms engaged in work of this kind the grammar school boy was ready at fifteen, sixteen or seventeen years of age to go to the University.

Beginning as a group or corporation of students who gathered round some notable scholar, a university came to mean a recognised association of students or of masters under the protection and later under the control, to a certain extent, of some civil authority.

From the 13th and 14th centuries onward the universities seem to have made a stronger appeal to men's imagination and sympathy than the monasteries and the endowment of colleges went on apace. Church-statesmen, sovereigns, private individuals bequeathed large sums for this purpose, and the colleges thus founded were under the control of the Founder's statutes and later under a certain measure of state control also, and after the Reformation, when the connection between State and Church became so close, the Church control which had always been acknowledged became very much increased so that the Church

---

[1] Brinsley's *Ludus Literarius* gives an excellent idea of the grammar school in the 17th century.

dominated both the grammar schools and the universities.

The students who went up to the universities from the grammar schools were, as a rule, the younger sons whose small patrimony made earning a living essential and who therefore required professional training. As has been seen the grammar schools were supposed to teach the trivium, but as a matter of fact they gave instruction generally only in grammar, rarely in rhetoric and never in logic. Indeed, often a Founder of a College was compelled to provide for the completion of the grammar school course before a student could attend with advantage the university lectures. Walter de Merton arranged for a master of grammar in Merton College to teach poor boys and to help the undergraduates who ' were to go to him in any difficulty without any false shame[1].'

Having perfected himself in Latin, the young undergraduate proceeded to the study of logic and rhetoric so as to become a disputant in the schools—a much more formidable task than reading a theme in a grammar school. After three years' training he was ready for his ' Determination ' a public disputation at the end of which he received his B.A. degree. Then, a trained disputant, he was ready to enter upon his four years' course in the quadrivium (arithmetic, geometry (including geography), music and astronomy), prior to

[1] Rait, *Life in the Mediæval University*, p. 34, and see also p. 58. ' Wm. of Wykeham in providing for the needs of his scholars availed himself of the experience of the past and created a new model for the future. The Fellows of New College were to be efficiently equipped at Winchester (grammar school) for the studies of the University.'

his inception as a Master of Arts when he received a licence and, in some periods, a command to teach. After the completion of this general course he was free to take up specialised study in theology, law, or medicine.

This suggests a really liberal education ; but two facts must be remembered, first that the work of a lecturer was merely to read to more or less attentive students the accepted treatises on the various subjects —interpretations and comments might be added if the lecturer was desirous of making a reputation ; and second that almost the whole strength of the students went to the endless disputes about the veriest trifles. This is of course tantamount to saying that the universities aimed first, at the training of a disputant who should possess, in the highest degree, the art of producing the subtlest refinements upon the arguments of his predecessors or rivals and secondly, at training clergymen, lawyers and doctors. Many students however did not pass to the second stage, and the subjects of the quadrivium were chiefly useful in furnishing illustrations for the disputations[1]. That these subjects had any bearing upon the realities of life and especially upon the individual life of the student was not for a moment suspected. With such aims there was almost as little change in curriculum and method in the universities as there was in the grammar schools.

At first this adherence to the same curriculum and

[1] ' The Quadrivium was of comparatively little importance ; Geometry and Music received small attention ; arithmetic and astronomy were at first chiefly useful for finding the date of Easter.' Rait, *Life in the medieval University*, p. 137.

to the same method for so many centuries seems inexplicable, especially when it is remembered that it persisted in spite of the enthusiasm of the Renaissance. As a matter of fact, however, there was more change owing to the Renaissance than is at first apparent. The interests awakened by the Renaissance were chiefly two ; first the interest in classical literature and second that in ' nature '—in man's physical environment. A third interest in man himself was present and influenced the other two but was not ' worked out ' until much later and does not specially concern us here. It was the interest in classical literature that first captivated men's imagination and enthusiasm. Every historian of the Renaissance in Italy describes the eagerness with which search was made for original MSS. and the zeal with which those which were discovered were read, copied and passed from university to university to awaken in each increased devotion to the study of the ancient world. A later stage was reached when, instead of reading these texts to discover the knowledge possessed by the Ancients and their opinions and ideals, students pored over them to note differences in style and construction. Later, enthusiasts began to produce textual notes and to set up as their ideal as close and perfect an imitation of classical authors, and especially of Cicero, as possible. From that time a narrowing to formalism was inevitable. The very eagerness of the Humanists was the seed-plot of Ciceronianism. The resultant effect in the schools was two-fold. First it was classical and not ecclesiastical Latin that was studied, and second, grammar was taken more and more as a subject in itself existing apart from any text. Evidence of this is seen in the large number of new grammars which were written and in the regulations which appeared in the Charters of new schools as to the grammar to be used[1]. It will readily be understood that to study the contents of the classical texts ; to attempt to give instruction in the subjects of which they treated, such as history, geography and astronomy, demanded a willingness to change and an enthusiasm which were the possession of the few ; while to give an increased amount of grammar, a more thorough memory training and drilling in theme-writing, was but to require a steadier and a more settled continuance in the old, narrow ways.

The second great interest of the Renaissance period was that in the world of nature. This was awakened owing very largely to a gradually conceived idea of the Greek joy in life and in nature and also owing to the many scientific discoveries of the period. For a time, this second interest was overshadowed by the rapid development of the enthusiasm for classics ; but little by little it grew and slowly influenced the old quad-rivium, the subjects of which became more and more differentiated. It would seem then that the universities ought to have been affected ; but the earliest influence here was, as in the grammar schools, exerted by the zeal for the classics. ' New Learning ' at Oxford and Cambridge meant classical Latin and Greek. In

[1] See Eton time-table (supra p. 6) which mentions, as well as the famous grammar of Lily, the Stanbridge grammar. Stanbridge was a schoolmaster at Banbury about 1500. He made his school so celebrated by his teaching that the statutes of new schools often required the master to teach ' grammar after the manner of Banbury school.'

the universities, too, the sanctity of tradition proved too powerful even for such men as Erasmus, Linacre and others.   That new subjects were introduced is undoubtedly true, but their adoption was entirely fortuitous and the teaching of the subject invariably ceased with the removal of the teacher.   Moreover, after the Reformation, Church control was practically synonymous with State control and the Tudors, finding that too much of the ' New Learning ' led to the spread of Puritanism in the universities and to a dangerous love of theological arguments, confined the work there to rigidly defined theological courses.   As Mr Mullinger says of the reign of Elizabeth—' It had been decided that Cambridge should be mainly a school of divinity and that the doctrine taught in her schools should be defined and prescribed beforehand... The main interest having centred in the discussion of theological questions whatever was taught of liberal learning sank to an almost lifeless tradition[1].'

Tradition therefore, supported by authority in the hands of the Church, decided that both in grammar schools and universities there should be faithful adherence to the old ways—to the provision of a classical training for the servants of the Church.   But however strong they might be, tradition and authority could not prevent the working out of the great conceptions that had their birth at the Renaissance.   However narrow the schools and universities might become, there were still men who clung to the hope that Humanism would ultimately triumph.   As early as the first half of the 16th century scorn was poured upon the Ciceronian

[1] *History of Cambridge University*, p. 134.

teaching in the writings of Erasmus and Rabelais, while Montaigne's *Essay on Pedantry* was published in 1580. In our own country Sir Thomas Elyot, in his ' Boke named the Governour ' which was published in 1531, wrote very strongly against the narrow humanists. ' And who that hath nothinge but language only,' he writes, ' may be no more praised than a popinjay, a pye or a stare whan they speke featly...wherefore they be moche abused that suppose eloquence to be only in wordes or coulours of Rhetorike...undoubtedly very eloquence is in every tonge where any matter or acte done or to be done is expressed in wordes clene, propise, ornate and comely[1].' Here, Elyot, notable already for having had the courage to write in English[2], not only writes against the excessive drilling in language, *i.e.* in grammar and in training in eloquence, but says it is possible to express one's self in one's own language and that everyone does not need to spend long years in the study of Latin only. The course which he proceeds to sketch for the gentleman is very broad and includes all the ' modern ' subjects advocated by the early Humanists—geography, history, astronomy, and the rest—and not only has physical education an important place but painting, carving and such subjects are to be included. Elyot's suggestions are typical of those made not only in England but in Italy and France too during the 16th century when there was an effort to combine the broad humanistic scholarly training with the mediaeval knightly training

---

[1] *The Governour.* Everyman Edition, pp. 54 and 55.

[2] Compare J. L. Vives who certainly advocated the use of the vernacular and yet wrote in Latin—*De Tradendis Disciplinis.*

and to produce the scholar-gentleman. That this was the ideal to be aimed at during the Tudor period is abundantly clear from a consideration of the life at Elizabeth's court ; Sidney, Raleigh, Leicester and many others were perfect embodiments of this conception[1].

This broader education with its recognition of physical needs and its practical bearing upon life appealed strongly to the new Tudor nobility who loved a much fuller life than was possible in the excessively ecclesiastical atmosphere of the colleges of Oxford and Cambridge.

It was just the nobles moreover who, free from the authority of Church or State and untrammelled by tradition, could obtain, either at home under their tutors or abroad in the courtly Academies, which arose in France[2], this new education. In England too attempts were made to supply the new need. At the Inns of Court a practical and physical education was obtainable and in 1571 Sir Humphrey Gilbert drew up a scheme for an academy similar to those in France. The work in this Academy was to be provided for as follows : ' For Latin, Greek, one schoolmaster and four ushers ; a teacher of Hebrew ; also one for logic and rhetoric ; one teacher for moral philosophy and one in natural philosophy and a reader in physic. The last-named two were required to conduct experiments and were afforded a " physic-garden " for the purpose.

[1] Castiglione's *Il Cortegiano*, translated into English by Sir Thomas Hoby in 1561, influenced the development in this direction in England, and Peacham's *Compleat Gentleman* of 1622 is on the same lines.

[2] Mentioned by many English writers—Lord Herbert of Cherbury and John Evelyn among others.

The rest of the staff included a reader of civil law and one for divinity ; a lawyer for grounds of the Common Law...one teacher of French (with an usher) ; one of Italian (with an usher) ; one of Spanish ; one of the High Dutch, *i.e.* German ; one master of defence ; of dancing and vaulting ; of music (with an usher) ; one herald of arms, and a teacher of riding the Great Horse ...These subjects were to be taught in English and text-books in English were to be encouraged[1].'

This Academy and a few others on the same plan aimed at giving a ' modern ' education to the nobility— they, unfettered by Church and State control, were at liberty to arrange their education as they wished. Travel at that time played an important part in the education of a gentleman, and with the rise of ver- nacular literatures it is not surprising to find that provision was made for English to be used and for modern languages to receive attention. Probably the most notable feature of the curriculum is the natural philosophy and physic and the injunction that a physic garden was to be provided. That the ' modern ' educa- tion of those days included instruction in the Sciences was chiefly due to the influence of Peter Ramus (1515– 1572) whose ' most fundamental and far-reaching con- tribution ' to the development of educational theory ' was his aid to the emancipation of society from the bondage to mediaeval authority and to the enfranchise- ment of truth and free investigation[2].'

Ramus began his attack upon the philosophical and

---

[1] Quoted from *The Beginnings of the Teaching of Modern Subjects in England*, by Foster Watson. Introd. p. xxxii.

[2] Graves, *Peter Ramus*, p. 204.

educational method of his day by maintaining as the thesis for his M.A. degree the astonishing proposition ' All that Aristotle has said is false.' This was in 1536. It is difficult for us to grasp the full significance of this event. When it is remembered that all the labours of the schoolmen were based upon an unquestioning acceptance of the method laid down by Aristotle ; that should Aristotle be proved wanting all the toil of the Middle Ages would be of no avail ; in other words, that if Ramus were right then all the disputations of every professor and every student in every university in Europe would be valueless—when this is remembered it will be seen what tremendous import his argument had. It was in vain that men said that, but for Aristotle, Ramus would not have been able even to dispute ; the fact remained, he had dared to question and even to denounce, not merely an authority but the only authority. This was the beginning of a life spent in devotion to educational reform. He first set himself to show the true value of logic and to expound the right method of knowledge. He was, of course, ardently opposed to Ciceronianism, and as a result of his work the curriculum gradually underwent an improvement. He very much simplified the subjects of the trivium and aimed at making the teaching of language easier. But it was the subjects of the quadrivium that were especially influenced ; as Graves says ' He improved all literary and expression studies and helped to give mathematics and science a start[1].' At first there was the inevitable storm of opposition to the Innovator—a person to be avoided in those days ;

[1] *Peter Ramus*, p. 218.

but gradually many scholars in the great universities realised that Aristotelian philosophy—or at least, the mediaeval conception of it was inadequate—and that adherence to mediaeval methods was responsible for the slow growth of knowledge. The result was that before long a new idea took shape—that if only a right method could be adopted not only would men's knowledge increase but with the spread of knowledge would vanish the social evils of the day. The first desideratum was the increase of knowledge. Gradually, in practically every country in Western Europe were found men who accepted the new philosophy—Ramism, as it was called, and having substituted the ' method of experience ' for reliance upon authority, set themselves to prosecute vigorous inquiries into every branch of knowledge. The Geometry of Euclid[1] and Mathematics generally were eagerly studied ; astronomy was developed ; natural philosophy and physics gradually divided up into medicine, anatomy, botany, and physics.

Closely connected with the desire to add to the sum of human knowledge was the wish to apply that knowledge to the augmentation of the sum of human happiness. It was in North Europe especially that Humanism developed an interest in social questions and in this, of course, it was allied with the Reformation. Ramus, who became a Protestant, was as eager as anyone to ameliorate social conditions, and his educational reforms were inspired very largely with the desire to bring education into line with the social needs of the day and to place it within the reach of every one.

[1] Ramus' *Geometry*, founded on Euclid was published 1596.

During the latter half of the 16th century, then, two streams of thought may be traced ; one concerned with the development of science—with the study of natural phenomena ; the other concerned with the attempt to modify education in accordance with economic changes and to give some education to every individual. In the 17th century both these tendencies were recognised by Comenius who undertook the task of noting the trend of public opinion and of formulating educational theories in accordance therewith. But Comenius must be dealt with later. In the meantime the attitude of Englishmen to these two tendencies must be noted.

England took no small share in the development of Science and, as we have seen, the nobles were eager in the pursuit of the new subjects which formed part of the curriculum of the Courtly Academies. It is curious to note that in Sir Humphrey Gilbert's scheme no branch of mathematics is included, though, owing to the geometry by Ramus which was translated into English by Thomas Hood in 1590, the subject became more widely studied, especially by Cambridge scholars. The acceptance of Ramism by these scholars at Cambridge prepared the way for the work of later mathematicians and especially for that of Newton. It is probable that Bacon, who later followed Ramus in his examination of Aristotelian philosophy, came under the influence of Ramism at Cambridge. At Oxford, too, some interest was being taken in mathematics ; the founder of the Savilian professorship, Sir Henry Savile, lectured in his subject about 1570. But as was the case when Erasmus taught Greek at Cambridge at the beginning of the 16th century, the teaching was casual and cannot be said to have formed a definite part of the University course or to have in any but the slightest way influenced the general attitude of the University to the new subject.

When inquiry is made as to the progress of the sciences it is found that they developed independently of the support of the University as such. It is true that in this branch also advanced men strove to awaken the authorities to the trend of the times ; but without much result. For example, a physic garden was opened in Oxford in 1632 and was designed to be of special service in the medical course, while Antony Wood records that on April 23, 1663, he ' began a course of chimistry under the noted chimist Peter Sthael of Strasburgh.' These chemistry lectures to a ' club which consisted of ten at least ' were probably the first that had been given in Oxford and were of course quite unconnected with the University. Sthael, a Lutheran was taken to Oxford by Robert Boyle in 1659 and ' began to take to him scholars in the house of John Cross next on the west side to University College where he began but with three scholars[1].' Wood gives the names of several of those who attended the lectures, among them were Dr J. Wallis, Mr Christopher Wren and Dr Ralph Bathurst ; he also records that the ' Chimical Club ' which he joined concluded on May 30th, 1663, ' And A.W. paid Mr Sthael 30 shillings, having in the beginning of the class given 30 shillings beforehand,' and then he makes this comment ' A.W. got some knowledge and experience but his mind

[1] *Life and Times of Antony Wood* (Oxf. Hist. Soc.), I. p. 472.

still hung after antiquities and music[1].'   In the next year Sthael went to London to become the ' operator of the Royal Society ' and continued in that position for the next seven or eight years.   It was the group of men who meeting in London[2], in the years following 1645, and spoken of often as the ' invisible College ' and the Oxford group of ' 48–50 '—Wilkins of Wadham, Bathurst, Wren, Wallis and for some time Boyle and Petty and others—who about 1660 organised their meetings and formed the Royal Society.   From that time it was the Royal Society and not the universities which became the centre of the scientific movement and to which all the scientific discoveries were reported. It must not be forgotten, of course, that all scientific studies were regarded as more or less closely connected with the Black Art, and the theologians still harboured something of the spirit which in earlier days had declared Galileo a heretic.   In the 17th century many considered not only scientists but mathematicians also as Atheists and the professors of them ' limbs of the devil[3],' and therefore it is not to be wondered at that the universities, the strongholds of ecclesiastical feeling, should regard with suspicion the new learning and that the members of the Royal Society had for years to endure ridicule and censure.   The work of the Royal

[1] *Life and Times of Antony Wood*, p. 475.

[2] Sometimes at Gresham College, founded under the will of Sir Thomas Gresham (1519–1579).   He endowed professorships in divinity, astronomy, music, geometry, law, medicine and rhetoric ; he encouraged the use of practical methods and required the teaching to be in English and not in Latin.   The work of Gresham College was therefore more utilitarian and realistic than that in the universities.

[3] Antony Wood's *Athenae Oxon.* II. p. 336.

Society may be described as serious and scientific in the strict sense of the word ; in other quarters there were attempts made to keep abreast of the times in the study of science, and books containing descriptions of animals and of collections of rarities of all kinds were published. This is of course merely the first stage in the development of any science ; but these books, under the general influence of the time, had often a strong scriptural and ethical tone. This type of book is represented by such a work as that of Samuel Purchas, ' A theatre of flying insects where especially the nature, worth and work, wonder and manner of the right ordering of the bee is discovered and described with theological, historicall and morall observations[1].' As Mr Foster Watson shows in his *Beginnings of the Teaching of Modern Subjects in England* books of this kind probably influenced some schoolmasters and occasionally, therefore, some attempt would be made to improve the curriculum. Desires of this nature are seen not only in the work of an advanced schoolmaster here and there like Hezekiah Woodward, who advocated nature study for schools, or John Dury, but in the numerous pamphlets and addresses which appeared in the first half of the 17th century—an age of pamphlets and of all manner of schemes for the amelioration of the conditions of the people.

There is no doubt that with the rise of Puritanism the 16th century saw a strengthening and a crystallising into definite shape of the Reformation ideal of

[1] Foster Watson, *Beginnings of the Teaching of Modern Subjects in England*, note p. 189.

the recognition of the worth of the individual. This resulted in the growth among the people of England not only of a desire to exercise their reason with regard to religious questions or even to obtain a measure of control over the government, but also of a firm conviction of the need for universal education. To think of the leaders of the Commons of England in the 17th century as being interested in religious and constitutional questions without recognising that they grasped the importance of sound universal education is not to do justice to the breadth and enlightenment of their views. Moreover, just as they strove to obtain a reformed church and a reformed method of government, so they laboured to bring about a reformed education. The worthless, formal grammar grind of the schools was criticised almost as strenuously as the formalism of the Church, and it is not too much to say that as there were two parties (broadly speaking) in the Church, so there were two parties in the schools, one satisfied in continuing to give the old classical training, the other wishing to introduce new methods and new subjects. And the members of the ' reforming ' party in the schools were generally to be found among the ' reforming ' party in the Church ; for the Puritans, driven by persecution to Holland and Switzerland, had there come into contact with the strongest forces making for progress, and in the Protestant centres of learning under the stimulating guidance of such men as Cordier, Bérauld and Calvin had been much influenced by the new philosophy. Eager in the pursuit of the new knowledge which was rapidly opening out, the Puritans were enthusiastic also in their determination to apply the great principle enunciated by Bacon, that since observation (use of the senses) is the true way to learning (and not scholastic philosophy) everyone can, with the aid of the right method, be taught everything. Probably the most enthusiastic worker along these lines among the Puritans[1] was Samuel Hartlib, a Polish merchant, who seems never to have done any business, and who, a refugee, came to England about 1628 and remained here until after the Restoration, when he seems to have gone to Holland. During the whole time he was engaged in trying to set on foot various philanthropic schemes so that Milton, one of his many friends, wrote of him as ' a person sent hither by some good Providence from a far country to be the occasion and incitement of great good to this island.' Hartlib appears to have been a gentle lovable man with as many friends as enthusiasms. Writing to Dr Worthington, Master of Jesus College, Cambridge, he says ' I could fill whole sheets in what love and reputation I have lived these thirty years in England being familiarly acquainted with the best of Archbishops, Bishops, Earls, Viscounts, Barons, Knights, Esquires, Gentlemen, Ministers, Professors of both Universities, merchants and all sorts of learned or in any kind useful men etc.[2]' The last phrase is significant. Hartlib seems to have spent his time making the acquaintance of and corresponding with learned men and particularly with men interested in

---

[1] The term is used loosely to cover Independents, Presbyterians, Lutherans, etc.—all extreme ' low ' churchmen.

[2] Quoted in *Biographical Memoir of S. Hartlib* by G. H. Dircks, p. 4.

new subjects, in inventions and in philanthropic schemes, as Masson says ' nothing of a hopeful kind with novelty in it came amiss to Hartlib[1].' For years he corresponded with Robert Boyle and a characteristic letter to him in 1649 shows him ready to help another scientific inquirer—' My endeavours are now how Mr Petty may be set apart and encouraged for the advancement of experimental and mechanical knowledge in Gresham College in London.' That Hartlib was imbued with the spirit of his time is abundantly evident. He was filled with enthusiasm about the wonderful discoveries that were being made ; ready to sympathise with Petty in his excitement about a machine for double writing he had invented ; eager to tell John Evelyn of improvements in German stoves. In fact, anyone interested in things of this kind was sure to find in Hartlib not only a man ready to listen but a friend ready to help by arranging for the publication of a pamphlet which should introduce some new marvel to the general public. He seems indeed to have been in himself a kind of ' Office of Public Address' and thus to have actually for his own circle of friends put into execution one of his most cherished schemes. Among his multifarious interests the chief were religion and education and these brought him into close friendship with two men devoted to both causes—John Dury and John Amos Comenius. It was Dury's life work to bring about a reconciliation of the Calvinists and Lutherans, and in fact a union of all the Protestant churches of Europe on some broad basis which could be accepted by all. It was Hartlib's

[1] Masson, *Life of Milton*, Vol. III. p. 215.

part to publish various letters and pamphlets and to introduce them and Dury to influential people who might be expected to further the project. These endeavours brought both men into close contact with Comenius, an exiled Moravian bishop, and the bond of union between the three was further strengthened by the fact that very dear to each of them was the problem of social and of educational reform. It was Comenius who was destined through his writings to have the greatest influence on the development of education. Alive to the philosophic thought of his day he became the great exponent of Realism in educational theory. During the silence enforced upon him, as a minister, by persecution, he applied himself to the task of becoming acquainted with books on education and to the formulation of a new theory which should be based upon a recognition of the need for a useful and practical as well as for a universal education. He himself, as he tells us, had suffered in a grammar school one of ' those slaughter houses of the young ' and he laboured therefore first, to reform the methods in use there. He became for a time head of the Gymnasium at Lissa, and his experience as a teacher led him to issue simplified Latin school texts which soon became known in every country in Europe. As early as 1633 knowledge of Comenius had reached England ; for in that year Thomas Horne, M.A., a schoolmaster in London, and then Master of Eton, had published a *Janua Linguarum* which is said by Antony Wood to have been mostly taken from Comenius—the title is his at any rate. But it was Hartlib who was really to make Comenius known in this country—it was possibly he who had introduced his texts to the notice of Horne and others. Whether this was so or not, in 1637 we find Hartlib publishing *Preludes of the Endeavour of Comenius from the Library of S.H., Oxford.* There is first a preface to the reader and then the treatise—' Porta Sapientia Reserata etc.— the Gate of Wisdom opened or the Seminary of all Christian knowledge ; being a new compendium and solid method of learning more briefly, more truly and better than hitherto, all the sciences and arts and what- ever there is manifest or occult that it is given to the genius of man to penetrate, his craft to imitate, or his tongue to speak. The author that Rev. and most dis- tinguished man, Mr J. A. Comenius.' The story of this publication is told by Comenius himself. Hartlib, it seems, had heard of Comenius' plan for a large work dealing with an educational system which should pro- vide not only for an improved method of teaching languages, but also for a method of teaching ' things.' Comenius was begged by Hartlib to give him a sketch of this intended ' Janua Rerum.' ' Being thus en- treated ' says Comenius, ' by the most intimate of my friends, a man piously eager for the public good, to communicate some ideas of my future work, I did communicate to him in writing in a chance way what I had thought of prefixing sometime or other to the work in the form of a preface and this, beyond my hope and without my knowledge was printed at Oxford under the title of *Conatuum Comenianorum Pracludia*[1].' The pamphlet gives an idea of the realistic position. Start- ing with the conviction that ' nothing is in the under- standing which was not before in the senses ' the

[1] Quoted in Masson's *Life of Milton.*

realists proposed to replace the old memory and language training—mere ' words '—by a training of the understanding through the cultivation of the powers of observation. Lessons about real things were to be given, illustrations were to be used and above all the subject was to be approached from the point of view of the child's limited capacity for understanding. The realists were ' encyclopaedists ' also ; for, since the senses were the gate-way to knowledge, a training of the senses would bring all knowledge within the grasp of the child, and therefore there was no subject which at some stage he might not learn.

Though Comenius was no doubt somewhat annoyed by Hartlib's over-zealousness, their friendship was not broken, for in 1641 Comenius was induced to come to England for the purpose of putting into practice some of his educational theories. No doubt Hartlib's publication had helped to increase his already great reputation in England, and Comenius writes as though he had been invited by Parliament. Whether the invitation was sent by Parliament or not is not known ; but it is certain that there were many teachers and many influential friends of Hartlib exceedingly anxious to reform English education with the help of the acknowledged leader of education in Europe. The plan was to arrange for the opening of a realistic College in London which should give a scientific—an encyclopaedic, education based on the new methods enunciated by Bacon and Comenius. It was felt that to attempt anything of this kind at Oxford or Cambridge, which were so embedded in Ciceronianism, would be futile. Besides, the new education was to be utilitarian and was to appeal not only to professional but to commercial and middle class men generally, so that London was a better centre than the ancient universities would be. There was, moreover, more probability of success for the new education in a College on a fresh foundation than in the universities which could not be expected to welcome studies so little in keeping with the mediaeval atmosphere which still hung about them. This visit is of very great importance ; it shows unmistakably the great interest taken in education on the eve of the Civil War. Unfortunately the outbreak of that war prevented Hartlib and his friends from making use of Comenius as they had hoped, but that does not mean that the visit was a failure. The fact remains that it was to England that the great educational reformer was invited ; that so early as in the first half of the 17th century there was a great desire to establish here the new education ; that the opening of a College giving expression to the ideas of Bacon and Comenius was thought to be so well within the bounds of possibility that sites were discussed. Too much emphasis cannot be placed upon this scheme ; it goes to prove that England was in the forefront of educational reform and it was moreover the beginning of a realistic movement which, though interrupted for a time, never really died down.

While Comenius was in England, Hartlib published once more his views on the reformation of schools. During the months that Comenius was here Hartlib must have been a happy man. To have the great educationalist of the day staying with him ; to be able to introduce Comenius to sympathetic friends ; to be constantly arranging gatherings for the discussion of their pet theories—how Hartlib must have revelled in all this ! And what an influence the visit was destined to have ! When Comenius went away it is true no Pansophical College had been opened in London to give a realistic education far in advance of that given at Oxford or Cambridge ; but there were left behind men more determined than ever to leave no stone unturned to further their aims.

Hartlib was as active as ever ; in 1644 at his earnest request, Milton, who had been teaching his two nephews and a few other boys since 1639, wrote his views on education. The *Tractate* is too well known to need much comment. In it Milton repeats the criticism of the current university and grammar school methods which is to be found in all advanced writers of the period, and is quite in agreement with Comenius in his desire to give a realistic education. Unlike Comenius, who planned a complete system of national education beginning with the school of the mother's knee, followed by the vernacular school which led on to the grammar school and university, Milton dealt with the education of upper class children only, and, ignoring the elementary system, wrote only of secondary work. He suggests an academy in which both grammar school and university education should be given ; he wished indeed to do away with the established universities entirely. Here of course he is but voicing the general feeling of the Puritans—that Oxford and Cambridge were so averse to anything new that the only hope of effecting a change was to set up rival universities which should from the first devote themselves to giving expression to realism. This feeling of the Puritans was so openly expressed that Antony Wood writes of the ' endeavours to pull down Academies '—' It is well knowne ' he writes in 1659, ' that the Universities of this land have had their beginnings and continuances to noe other end but to propagate religion and good manners and supply the nation with persons chiefly professing the three famous faculties of Divinity, Law and Phisick. But in these late times when the dregs of people grew wiser than their teachers and...therefore above[1] all religion ordinarily profest, nothing could satisfie their insatiable desires but aiming at an utter subersion of them[2], church and schools....Intelligent men knew and saw verie well that it was their intent to rout up all and to ruine those things that smelt of an Academy, never rejoycing more then when they could trample on the gowne and bring humane learning and arts into disgrace. This I may verie boldlie say and none can denye it that these domestick confusions among ourselves about matters of religion and insurrections of seditious subjects that have and doe pretend to reformation, hath bin the only reasons why these nurseries must first feele the smart of their implacasy....And as it was a common matter to declaime against universities in publicke, soe was it also in the private meetings and conventicles of Anabaptists, Quakers and such like unstable people, challenging also sometimes the gowne itself to oppose what they did and said and this ever in the universities themselves[3].'

Here, no doubt, Wood is referring to the extremists

[1] *i.e.* ' superior to.'　　　　[2] The universities.
[3] Wood's *Life and Times*, Vol. I. pp. 292, 293.

who, now and then, were concerned to show ' The sufficiency of the Spirit's teaching without Humane Learning.' This is the title of a ' Treatise tending to prove Humane Learning to be no help to the spiritual understanding of the word of God ' written by a cobbler, S. How. As a matter of fact two separate controversies raged. Puritan extremists of How's type contended that ministers did not require much education and considered the universities not merely useless but harmful. Milton in his *Likeliest means to remove hirelings out of the Church* had some slight share in this discussion. He saw no need for the training of ministers in disputations and regarded the time spent at the universities as wasted, because so little was gained there. ' A minister can receive his education,' he writes, ' at any private house instead of at the university. Else to how little purpose are all these piles of sermons, bodies and marrows of divinity besides all other sciences in our English tongue—many of the same books which in Latin they read in the University ? ' It was not an educated ministry to which Milton objected—far from it ; it was against the waste of time and the bad methods at the universities that he wrote. And this was the burden of the writings of those who took part in the larger controversy which dealt with the question of the value of such training as was given in the universities. The general body of the Puritans did not wish, as Wood suggests they did, to sweep away all learning, but they did desire to get rid of all narrowness in the universities and also of all negligence and supineness[1].

[1] The Wood collection of pamphlets in the Bodleian contains

The account which Wood himself gives of the university of Oxford during the Commonwealth shows that so far from doing away with education, the Presbyterians and Independents who during the ' Intervall ' filled the colleges, were earnest hard-working men who did their utmost to promote sound learning.

But to return to Milton. The account which Edward Phillips gives of his uncle's teaching shows that Milton wrote from a knowledge of what might be done and that he went a great way in the accomplishment of what he suggested. Apparently Milton hoped to develop his small Academy and to carry out his theories, but in 1647 he had to discontinue his teaching. There is no reason to suppose, however, that his interest in education diminished. As time went on he became more at one in his opinions with Cromwell, and no doubt the Protector and his Latin Secretary were often associated in educational schemes.

Meanwhile Hartlib continued to publish pamphlets. One issued in 1645 by his young friend William Petty deserves notice. Born in 1623 Petty received the usual grammar school education, ' at 12 he had acquired a competent smattering of Latin.' Then he was apprenticed as cabin boy on an English merchantman[1] but having broken his leg he was put ashore in France not

one by Mat. Poole ' A model for the maintaining of students of choice abilities at the University and principally in order to the ministry ' it is followed by an address (a ' begging ' letter) ' To the Rich that love Christ, the Church, the Gospel and themselves ' and pleads the need of a learned ministry. It is signed Richard Baxter (1658).

[1] It was a common practice to apprentice boys in this way as a means of continuing their education. Sir Thomas Gresham had been apprenticed to his uncle, a merchant in the Levant.

far from Caen. Here his smattering of Latin procured him entrance to a Jesuit College where he received further instruction in grammar ; picked up French ; and supported himself by teaching navigation to an officer and English to a French gentleman. After returning to England for a short time, he entered the Navy and in 1643 joined the army of the English refugees in the Netherlands where he ' vigorously followed his studies especially that of medicine at Utrecht, Leyden and Amsterdam[1].' Two years later he was in Paris studying anatomy and, in 1648 after the reorganisation of the University by Parliament, reaped the advantage of his studies in his appointment as deputy to Clayton, professor of anatomy, whom he succeeded as professor in January 1650. The note prefixed to the ' Advice of W. P. to Mr S. Hartlib for the Advancement of some particular parts of Learning ' in the *Harleian Miscellany* seems to suggest that one way of promotion was to address a pamphlet on education either to Parliament or to Hartlib. The note runs as follows—' Sir Wm. Petty having in 1644 invented an instrument for double writing obtained a patent from Parliament for the sole teaching of that art for seventeen years. Though this project (however promising in theory) did not turn to any great account in itself, yet by this means our author was brought into the knowledge of the leading men of those times ; and observing their proceedings at Oxford, he resolved to lay hold of the opportunity of fixing himself there. Having therefore written his " Advice to Mr H." he

---

[1] *Economic writings of Sir Wm. Petty*. C. H. Hull. Introd.

went thither in 1648 and became a great promoter of academical science.'

The pamphlet under discussion expresses contempt for traditional methods and advocates a realistic and utilitarian education. Petty suggests a ' literary workhouse where children may be taught to do something towards their living as (well as) to read and write ' ; indeed he urges that every child, even those of the highest rank, should be taught some genteel manufacture in their minority—such as making watches, painting, carving and embossing. In no case is drawing or designing to be omitted ; the elements of arithmetic and geometry are to be studied by all and such as ' have any natural ability and fitness to music[1] are to be encouraged and instructed therein.' The school should have in it a complete ' theatrum botanicum '— stalls and cages for all strange birds and beasts ; for ' children do most naturally delight in *things* and are most capable of learning them[2].'

In this pamphlet Petty is so concerned with advocating the new realistic or scientific education that he entirely breaks away from the old language curriculum. In this he is very different from Milton who retained not only humanistic studies such as history and literature but a thorough Latin training also. But Milton, and Comenius too, included the scientific branch of studies also. It is certainly unusual to find a writer who, like Petty, ignores the humanities—except to condemn excessive language teaching. Possibly the omission was not because Petty did not consider some

[1] Petty became Professor of Music at Gresham College.
[2] ' Advice of W. P. to Mr S. Hartlib,' *Harleian Misc.* p. 13.

language teaching necessary but because he knew it was safe to conclude that languages would assuredly be taught and because he felt it was imperative to concentrate his attention on the teaching of those new subjects which must have seemed so absolutely essential to an enthusiastic scientist.

The educational reforms of the period were chiefly concerned with two propositions, one dealing with a new method of teaching the classics, and the other with the introduction of new subjects. The two reforms were of course closely connected, and were based upon the corner-stone of Realism—' *things* not words.' Comenius, having urged the reform of grammar teaching by advising that the Latin words should be associated with the things for which they stood and which were represented by illustrations in his *Orbis Pictus*, went on to advocate the imparting of information about the things themselves. In the same way his followers in England passed naturally from advocating the use of what they called ' lively and vocal alphabets ' to the use of actual things in language lessons—' because some things cannot be pictured out with ink[1].' From this use in grammar lessons of pictures and things it was not far to lessons on the things themselves, *i.e.* to object lessons or ' nature study.' A noted schoolmaster friend of Hartlib's who introduced both these new ways in his school was the Puritan Hezekiah Woodward (1590–1675), who graduated B.A. from Balliol College, Oxford, 1612. After some time abroad, he opened a school at Aldermanbury

[1] Charles Hoole in his preface to his translation of the *Orbis Pictus* under the title of *The Visible World*, 1659.

in 1619. About 1649, having been for some years in sympathy with the Independents, he was presented by Cromwell to the vicarage of Bray near Maidenhead. He wrote several pamphlets on religious questions, but he was also intensely interested in education. Teaching experience, and remembrance of his own early useless education[1], soon led him to inquire into questions affecting method, and later to attempt reform. Charles Hoole, in his translation of Comenius's *Orbis Pictus*, refers to Woodward as an eminent schoolmaster, and his educational writings have the advantage of being the outcome of years of experience. Several books from his pen are important and prove him a realist in complete agreement with Comenius. Two pamphlets, written by him in 1641 and bound together, show him urging both the reforms mentioned above, they are ' A Light to Grammar and all other Arts and Sciences or the Rule of Practice, proceeding by the clue of nature and conduct of right reason so opening the doore thereunto,' and ' A Gate to Sciences opened by a naturale key or a Practicall lecture upon the great book of nature whereby the childe is enabled to read the creatures there.' In the former Woodward inquires into the nature of the child mind and says that hitherto teachers had thought only of the subject to be taught, he feels that grammar must be taught so as to be simple to the child—' hee that can stoope lowest and soonest fit his precognition to the child, he is the best teacher[2],' and he proceeds to advocate language teaching by a ' direct method ' with

---

[1] To which he refers in the preface to *Of the Child's Portion*.
[2] From the preface to *A Light to Grammar*.

plenty of illustration and explanation. The second pamphlet urges the teaching of science. In his prefatory letter to Hartlib, Woodward says 'The title tells us that all sciences are lighted into the understanding through the door of the senses and this is true enough for certaine it is that a child, yea a man also doth taste and relish no knowledge but what he finds drencht in flesh and blood.' There is no question that Realism had reached England and was, in some schools at least, making an onslaught upon Ciceronianism. Woodward was one of the most important schoolmasters to undertake measures for reform and in his struggles, and in the midst of the opposition of the Ciceronian schoolmasters was supported by Hartlib. This is not conjecture. A letter addressed to Hartlib forms the preface to *A Light to Grammar* and leaves one in no doubt as to Woodward's labours on the one hand and as to Hartlib's untiring efforts in encouraging any reformer, on the other. Woodward begins by thanking Hartlib for his encouragement, and after referring to the opposition of those who prefer the ' old, old way that is always the best way,' proceeds to sketch his attempts at reform. He then thanks Hartlib again saying ' since you came into these parts those discouragements about our school points began to weare out, such hath beene your activeness therein ; and which is the greatest meanes to make our way clearer you have been a meanes to make Comenius knowne amongst us, the greatest light in this kind of learning that ever was set up in the world. What, tho' the most will not think so—no wonder, that for the most judge all out of the way who drudge not on, just in the old road and beaten way[1].'

Enough has been said to show that Hartlib and his friends were anxious to reform, in these two directions of method and new subjects, the education given in the schools of their day. But Hartlib did not stop here. There was still another reform just as urgently needed. Hartlib seems to have felt more and more that the State should hold itself responsible for education which ought to be given to everyone. The idea that the giving of a thoroughly good, practical education to the middle classes is a matter of deep concern to the State, finds expression again and again in his own writings and in the ' advertisements ' or letters to the reader which he was in the habit of prefixing to the pamphlets he published for his friends. For instance, in his ' Considerations tending to the Happy Accomplishment of England's Reformation ' presented to Parliament in 1647 he mentions among the duties of magistrates that of seeing ' schools opened, provided with teachers, endued with maintenance, regulated with constitutions...and the right ordering of these schools is to be lookt upon as the main foundation of a reformed commonwealth without which no other work of reformation will ever bee effectual[2].' Again in his letter to the reader prefixed to John Dury's *Reformed School* he writes, ' the readiest way to reform both Church and Commonwealth is to reform the schools of education therein...and the way to reform these is to send

---

[1] Preface to *A Light to Grammar*.
[2] 'Considerations tending to the Happy...Reformation,' p. 21.

forth reformed schoolmasters[1].' This need for reformed schools and teachers was very strongly felt by
numbers of the Puritans, many of whom seem, according
to this letter by Hartlib, to have had an idea of forming
a community of men and women set apart to teach
boys and girls on the new lines. Dury's *Reformed
School* (1651) contains, in fact, the rules for the education of the boys in this projected institution, and the
care with which the scheme was thought out shows
the tremendous interest taken by the Puritans in
education. It may be said that this was only another
dream of Hartlib and Dury who spent their lives
making plans which could not be put into execution.
Possibly this is true ; both men were visionaries, and
there was probably no more possibility of this idea of
the Reformed Schools being carried out than there was
of Dury's scheme for a reconciliation of the Protestant
Churches being successful. But it at any rate shows
the direction in which these men's minds were working
and behind them were many sympathisers. There is
no doubt that the work of Hartlib and his immediate
circle was watched with interest not only by reforming
schoolmasters and advanced university men, who, finding no outlet for their activities in Oxford or Cambridge,
laboured with the Royal Society, but also by statesmen
too. Whether it be true or not that, as some believed,
Parliament invited Comenius to come to England to
advise Englishmen about education, it is true that, the
war being over, and the Commonwealth established, Parliament turned its attention to education. Grants were
made not only to the universities for the maintenance

[1] Preface to *Reformed School*, p. 4.

of the masterships of colleges and to Scotland for educational purposes but also to small necessitous schools and schoolmasters in different parts of the country[1]. A new university was planned for the North of England to be situated at Durham, and probably the scheme broached at the time of Comenius' visit to London was revived, for Gresham College and the meetings which developed into the Royal Society naturally suggested that there were good grounds for establishing a university in the capital.

The Commonwealth then, may be described as a time of considerable educational activity when men were big with hope for the future of learning. The work done between 1640–1660 was the natural outcome of the attempts made in those and the preceding years to influence public opinion in the direction of demanding educational reform. There is no doubt that the leaders among the Puritans were convinced of the importance of education and of the fact that without reform in education there could be no reform in the State. The majority of them had accepted the ' new education ' of the Realists and had quite definite ideas as to what reforms were necessary. They hoped that Realism would change existing institutions as much as possible, and that to counteract the influence of the universities and those grammar schools which remained Ciceronian, new institutions might be started. Men felt that the dream of Bacon and Comenius, and of the early Protestants indeed, was about to be realised, and

[1] See article on ' State and Education during the Commonwealth ' by Prof. Foster Watson in the *English Historical Review* for Jan. 1900 and see also A. F. Leach, *Educational Charters*, pp. 535–538.

that learning which had been the monopoly of the upper classes was at last within the reach of every individual who desired it. During the Commonwealth the door leading into the world of knowledge, of increased capacity, and of fuller life, was slowly opening to admit the men who stood expectant without. But just as they were on the threshold the door was shut —shut by the Restoration, and the way barred by the Clarendon Code.

Probably no event in English history has had so far-reaching and disastrous an effect upon education as the Restoration. Reform was put back nearly 200 years. After the return of Charles II there was the same attempt made to get rid of everything Puritan in education as in Church and State. Clarendon and his supporters understood only too well the Puritan demand for a reformed education. If Church and State were to be ' restored,' then education too must be ' restored.' If Church and State were to remain, they and they alone must control education. Puritans must be thrust out of the Church, realists—generally Puritans too—out of the schools. The very fact that so much attention was paid by the Restoration Parliament to education is evidence of the interest taken in it by the Puritans. Clarendon was plainly aware of the presence of a reforming party in the schools and he and his friends were as alarmed by the ' advanced ' views of many of the teachers as by those of some of the clergy. It was therefore felt that to secure uniformity of worship and belief, and the supremacy of the State-Church, independence of thought and action must be crushed in the school as well as in the Church ;

it was of no use requiring uniformity from preachers while leaving teachers free to spread new ideas which were so dangerously contemptuous of authority and tradition. No time was lost therefore in passing the Conformity legislation of 1662 and the following years —legislation which affected the schools and teachers no less than the churches and clergy. The effect on the churches is well known ; the effect on the schools was similar. From 1662 date the Dissenting churches ; from that year also date the Dissenting Academies. The Dissenting Academies gave not merely an education to Dissenters but a ' Dissenting ' education—an education that is, which was different from that in the other schools—an education which became much broader than that in the universities and in the schools established by law and controlled by the Church. As will be seen the ' Dissenting ' education was realistic ; for the Dissenters kept alive in their Academies the spirit of Hartlib and of those who had worked with him in the spread of realism.

II

THE RISE AND PROGRESS OF THE DISSENTING
ACADEMIES

When the complete History of Education in England appears, probably no chapter will cause more surprise to all students of education, except the few already interested in that time, than the one dealing with the period 1660–1800 which saw the rise of the Dissenting Academies.

These academies, diverging from the main stream of education, drained off more and more of its life and vigour until the parent stream grew weaker and weaker.

The change from the flourishing, energetic grammar schools of the 14th, 15th, and 16th centuries to the decaying lifeless ones of the 17th and 18th is so remarkable that it has been considered as the chief feature of the period, and the schools which make those years really interesting and noteworthy have been overlooked. The Dissenting Academies were, however, the greatest schools of their day. During a period when the grammar schools slept and when the universities were sterile the Dissenting Academies were not merely in existence, but were thoroughly alive and active, doing remarkably good work. In an age when those centres of learning to which men naturally turned for instruction, lamentably failed to fulfil the purpose of their founders, the Dissenting Academies did their utmost to satisfy the needs of the youth of this country, and an inquiry into the state of education between 1660 and 1800 shows us that they stood immeasurably higher, as regards efficiency, than any other educational institutions. The fact was soon recognised by men of their own day with the result that the academies trained men who filled the foremost places in every department of life, and that they eventually developed into the most important educational system of their day. Without the story of the Dissenting Academies the history of education in England for those 140 years would indeed be a dull and barren record ; as it is, these academies prevent those years from being a reproach to us ; for while other institutions were at a standstill they progressed, and it is therefore to them that the honour of furthering the development of educational opinion in this country belongs.

The Dissenting Academies were very largely the result of the Conformity legislation of 1662 and the following years ; that is to say, the passing of the Clarendon Code forced upon the Dissenters the execution of educational projects which had been in the minds of Puritans before 1660. The Act of Uniformity[1] provided that ' Every Schoolmaster keeping any public or private school and every person instructing or teaching any youth in any house or private family as a tutor or School master ' should subscribe a declaration

[1] For the complete text see *Documents relating to Act of Uniformity*, p. 391.

that he would conform to the liturgy as by law established and should also obtain a licence permitting him to teach from ' his respective archbishop, bishop or ordinary of the diocese.'

The effect of the Conformity legislation was to accentuate the differences between what may be called the orthodox State schools and the unorthodox Dissenting schools. Moreover, far from putting an end to the teaching of the Nonconformists, the Clarendon Code only served to give it that impetus which finally set the Dissenting schools far in advance of those—the grammar schools—under the control of the Church ; for it was not to be expected that Dissenters would offer no resistance to legislation which affected what they held to be so precious—liberty of conscience and a free liberal education. The ejected ministers and teachers were ready to fight for both. Of course, there was too, the practical side of the situation. These men had to obtain a living and consequently stern necessity was added to inclination, and therefore the determination was strengthened, with the result that further legislation, in the shape of the Five Mile Act of 1665, followed.

The fact that this Act was felt to be necessary only three years after the Act of Uniformity is in itself full of significance. The Act was most severe ; Nonconformists were forbidden to teach under the enormous penalty of £40, and the Act was very strictly enforced by both civil and ecclesiastical authorities. Archbishop Sheldon ordered the bishops to see whether ' said schoolmasters, ushers, schoolmistresses and instructors or teachers of youth publicly or privately

do themselves frequent the public prayers of the
Church and cause their " scholars " to do the same ;
and whether they appear well-affected to the government of His Majesty and the doctrine and discipline
of the Church of England[1].'

This increase of legislation and this diocesan in-
spection of teachers can mean only one thing—that
Dissenting Academies were even then becoming important. The reason is not far to seek. The Dissenting
Academies were supported and became important
because of three causes which operated quite naturally.
First, Nonconformist ministers and laymen would not
allow their sons to go to the universities where they
would have to subscribe the Act of Uniformity and
where they would be taught the doctrines for the
sake of which their fathers had left livings, professorships or tutorships. Secondly, just as the ejected
clergy were among the best in the country, so the
ejected teachers were among the most efficient and
progressive—the ejected teachers were, of course,
almost always clergymen. Reference to the list of
academies and tutors will show that the majority of
these men had been educated at a university and that
many of them in 1662 were fellows or tutors in Oxford
or Cambridge[2]. It will be clearly seen that in proportion as the Dissenting Academies profited by the good
work of the ejected teachers the grammar schools
lost, so that, as has been well said, ' the first result of
the Conformity legislation was the destruction of the

---

[1] de Montmorency, *The Progress of Education in England*, p. 46.
[2] Appendix No. I. Academies, Period I.

Elizabethan system[1].' This brings us to the third cause. It was not long before the effect of the legislation on the existing schools and on the universities was felt and people in those days were quite as anxious to get as good an education as possible for their money as they are to-day and therefore, in order to obtain a good education—the best education, in fact—Anglicans were very soon sent to the academies of the Dissenters which, requiring no oath of belief in any doctrine, were open to every one. The following extract from Wilson's ' History and Antiquities of Dissenting Churches and meeting houses in London, Westminster and Southwark ' is but one of a number which might be given to illustrate this : ' Mr Wm. Hocker received the rudiments of classical learning from Rev. Joseph Halfey ejected from the Rectory of St Michael Penkerel whose house, on its being known that for lack of a convenient school he had taken on himself the instruction of his own children, was thronged with gentlemen's sons of the first rank, though many of them were averse from Nonconformity.'

It was these three causes, then, which led to the immediate success of the Dissenting Academies. As time went on the Dissenters felt more secure and their work gained more and more recognition. This is what one would expect ; the severe legislation naturally led to a reaction which expressed itself in no uncertain manner in the judgment given in Bates' case, 1670, to the effect that if the schoolmaster were a nominee of the founder or of the lay patron of a school he could not be ejected for teaching without a Bishop's licence.

[1] de Montmorency, *The Progress of Education in England.*

Bates' case was a direct incentive to Dissenters to found schools. Evidence of the fact that advantage was quickly taken by the Dissenters of the pronouncement of the law-courts is shown by a table giving the dates when the endowed schools, in existence in 1851, were founded, which is given in Horace Mann's *Popular Education in Great Britain*—the official report of the Commission of Inquiry into Charities. The Commissioners reported 3000 endowed schools and of these nearly 1000 were founded between 1660–1730—these were of course chiefly elementary schools due not only to the effect of Bates' case but also to Cox's case, 1700, by which it was held that ' there was not and never had been any ecclesiastical control over any other than grammar schools ' ; to Douse's case which affirmed that it was not a civil offence to keep an elementary school without a bishop's licence; and to the Act of 1714 which exempted elementary schools from the penalties of the Conformity legislation[1].

But it is not with Dissenting schools in general that this book is concerned but with Dissenting Academies, a distinction which must be borne in mind. The Dissenting schools were charity foundations and probably differed little from the ordinary schools of the day. The Dissenting Academies on the other hand, were schools of university standing. That is to say that the academies were in the words of Toulmin ' Seminaries, which, but for a malignant policy would never have existed,' and which ' were opened in various parts of the kingdom to meet the wishes of such as would

---

[1] de Montmorency, *The Progress of Education*, p. 42.

otherwise have sent their sons to the Universities[1].'
There is clear evidence (from the lists of students with
dates of entry and from lives of eminent men who
received an academy education) which shows that boys
went to the academies at the age of 15, 16 or 17, *i.e.*
at the ordinary university age. Many names might be
given ; among them are : Belsham entered at Daventry,
and Chorlton at Rathmell when 15, Doddridge and
Caleb Ashworth both entered when 16, John Ashe
went to Rathmell when 16 ; some were older : Thos.
Dixon was 19 when he entered Chorlton's Academy,
Wm. Bull went to Daventry when 20 ; on the other
hand, Defoe and Calamy were only 14 when they went
to Newington Green and Cradock's Academy respectively. In a letter to the Rev. John Barker, Philip
Doddridge, D.D., Principal of the Academy at Northampton, writes that he does not generally take boys
who have not been through a grammar school and got a
good knowledge of classics.

Occasionally an explanation of the adoption of the
term Academy has been attempted. It has been
suggested[2] that the Dissenters used the term in con-
scious imitation of Calvin whose Academy established
at Geneva in 1559 was ' the first European University
not fortified by powers conveyed under a Papal Bull.'
It has been suggested also that in his choice of the
term Academy, Calvin, ' in thus invoking Plato who
taught in the olive grove of Academe,' wished to

---

[1] Toulmin's *Historical View of the State of the Protestant Dissenters
in England*, Vol. II. p. 217.

[1] In an address on *Early Nonconformity and Education* by
Principal Gordon.

proclaim his sympathy with Humanism and to empha-sise his breach with the Schoolmen. It is impossible to say how much truth there is in these suppositions ; they are certainly attractive to anyone dealing with the Humanism of the Dissenting Academies but they must not on that account be taken over without some examination.

There does not seem to be any evidence in support of the view that the term Academy was intended by Calvin to mean anything more than an institution at which higher education was obtainable. The word Academy was in general use at the time. It was considered as synonymous with university and was constantly employed to designate the great universities of Europe[1] or to indicate any institution giving in-struction in the subjects of the quadrivium. The instruction given by Sturm at Strasburg in the higher subjects received recognition when in 1562 the Emperor Maximilian II gave to the Gymnasium the right to grant degrees, and when, as a consequence, the Gym-nasium became known as an Academy.

As far as England is concerned the Dissenters were certainly not the first to apply the term to a place of higher education, for there are numerous instances of the same general use which obtained on the Continent. Antony Wood often speaks of Academies when re-ferring to the universities of Oxford and Cambridge ; Milton in the *Tractate* uses the term merely as equi-valent to university, to a place giving higher education ;

---

[1] This is shown by the titles of several books on the reform of the University of Paris by Ramus, *e.g. Pro philosophica Parisiensis Academiæ disciplina oratio.* Published 1551.

Sir Humphrey Gilbert, Bolton, Gerbier and others who endeavoured to introduce the education of the French courtly Academies into England clearly employed the term to indicate an institution giving instruction in the university subjects of the quadrivium.

The fact that the term Academy was widely used in Scotland, owing no doubt to the influence of Knox and Calvin, seems to give colour to the idea that the Dissenters were invoking Calvin as he is thought to have invoked Plato, and certainly the English Puritans were influenced by Calvin but they were also undoubtedly and to a very great extent influenced by their intercourse with Holland and Germany.

Possibly the term was used by the Dissenters to indicate that their work was of university and not of grammar school standard ; indeed the use of the term by Hartlib in 1660 to describe a school of a definitely realistic type may have suggested that ' Academy ' should be adopted as the name for these institutions which were so very different from the ordinary schools of the day. But it must after all be remembered that it is highly probable that in the early days the Dissenters themselves spoke of their schools or seminaries and not of their Academies.

An interesting parallel might be drawn between Calvin's Academy and the Dissenting Academies. Both were primarily for the training of ministers for the Church ; both were unorthodox, *i.e.* both gave an education in advance of their day and both were for a time brilliantly successful in meeting the demand for a new education. Inasmuch as the Dissenting Academies were at enmity with the ecclesiastical authority of their day and aimed at supplying an educated ministry for their own Church they may be considered as in line with Calvin's Academy, but except in so far as both Calvin's Academy and the Dissenting Academies in England were the outcome of Protestant enthusiasm for education there is no definite connection between them. On the Continent Protestant schools and Academies were founded as the result of a definite Protestant policy which aimed at the propagation of Protestant teaching. That these Protestant schools were important is seen from the fact that the Jesuit schools were founded to counteract their influence. In England there was no such general development, for after the Reformation all the Church schools and the universities became Protestant. With the Restoration and the Clarendon Code the Dissenters, cut off from the education supplied by Church and State, were compelled to provide for themselves and had no conception of the importance of the work they undertook and certainly no idea of establishing an educational system which should rival the universities.

The course in the academies usually extended over four years, and throughout the country it was understood that before entering, the students must have a general knowledge of classics. For example, in 1695, the Independent or Congregational Fund Board was established (1) to assist poor ministers, (2) to give young men who had already received a classical education, the theological and other training preparatory to the Christian ministry. Later, in 1730, the King's Head Society was founded by laymen in London who were dissatisfied with the management of the Fund

Academies. ' One chief point of objection was the rule which limited its students to those who had already passed through a classical training[1].' They resolved to found an academy with a six years' course, where young men, without a general classical education, would receive it during the first two years and could then proceed to the usual classical-theological course.

Naturally the theological course was the most important ; it was wide and included Divinity lectures, comprising the study of Greek and Hebrew and of the Jewish language and antiquities, Ethics, Natural Philosophy and Metaphysics. Lectures on sermon writing and pastoral care were also given and the sermons of Baxter, Tillotson, Charnock and others were read as models by the students. This work followed a training in Logic and Rhetoric which the theological students shared with those entered in other faculties[2].

---

[1] *Senatus Academicus*, p. 51.

[2] In his *Defence of the Academies* (against Samuel Wesley's attack) Palmer gives an account of the course at Bethnal Green where he was educated under Dr Kerr.   The 1st year time-table is shown in full ; Logic and some, if not all, of the Rhetoric were replaced by Metaphysics in 2nd year, Ethics in 3rd and Natural Philosophy in 4th.

Monday	Tuesday	Wednesday	Thursday	Friday	Saturday
Logic Rhetoric (Disputation)	Logic Rhetoric	Logic Rhetoric (Disputation)	Logic Rhetoric	Logic Rhetoric (Disputation)	Logic Rhetoric
1st year. Div. Lecture. [Buchanan's Psalm]					
Dinner Div. Gk. Test. Divinity Practical	Dinner Classics Div.Prac.	Dinner Classics Div. Prac.	Dinner Classics Div.Prac.	Dinner Div.Gk.Test. Div. Prac.	Dinner
2nd year. Metaphysics 3rd year. Ethics 4th year. Nat. Philo.					Sat. Morn. all superior classes declaimed by turns 4 & 4 on some noble & useful subject such as " De Pace."

The Dissenting Academies were not merely institutions of university standing, they were the rivals of the universities. No true conception of the greatness and importance of these academies can be formed unless it be clearly understood that though first starting practically even with the grammar schools they outstripped not only these schools in efficiency and influence, but having afterwards adopted university subjects and methods—moved to a higher plane as it were—they soon outstripped the universities also. They became, then, rivals who were acknowledged as such, not only by the general public who supported them, but by the university authorities who bitterly opposed them and did their utmost to ruin them. As a result, there were constant endeavours made to show that the tutors were preaching and teaching schism and resistance to civil law and the King. One of the most notable disputes in this connection was the Wesley-Palmer controversy[1]. This hostility on the part of the academies is referred to also in *More Short ways with Dissenters* where Defoe (educated at Newington Green Academy) says ' Open a door to us in your universities and let our youth be fairly admitted to study there without imposing oaths and obligations upon them and it shall no more be said that we erect schools in opposition to you.' The door remained closed ; but in spite of opposition, both civil and ecclesiastical, the academies prospered.

Though the Dissenting Academies became so very important, they were by no means large or numerous.

[1] See page 67 for full account of Wesley's remarks about academies.

Many of them were started by the ejected men, in their own homes, where they taught their sons and those of a few friends.

Some of the academies thus started lasted only a few years and died with their founder—of these the one at Islington under Ralph Button, M.A., 1672–1680, is an example. Owing to persecution under the Act of Uniformity and the Five Mile Act, the work was often interrupted ; some of the tutors suffered fine and imprisonment, and others had often to remove many times to out-of-the-way parts of the country. The academies were, therefore, very scattered, and as a consequence of this isolation they were carried on by men who had little or no communication with others similarly engaged, with the result that each academy had its individual characteristics. In attempting to form an idea of them and of the true nature of their work, one has to guard against taking what is recorded of one as applicable to all. In spite of this, however, features common to all can be discerned ; for though the tutors at their head acted separately with regard to details, yet they were one in spirit and aim and in the more important matters acted in accordance with the opinions of their co-religionists ; in the details of time-table they differed, in requiring no religious test and in general principles of teaching they agreed.

The academies may be divided into three classes, (1) those of the first period, 1663 to about 1690, founded by ejected ministers in which, as a rule, there was only one tutor, (2) those founded 1691–1750 in which there were several tutors and which were more ' public ' than the early ones and (3) those founded much later, about 1750, which gave, in addition to a professional training, a good general education to youths going into business[1].

The academies of the period 1663–1690 were ' private ' with usually about 20 or 30 students and only one tutor. Dissenters and Anglicans were trained together for the learned professions—the Church, Law and Medicine. The first period academies resembled the grammar schools, but showed a tendency to work on university lines, the tutors, university men, naturally employed all the methods already familiar to them[2]. Latin was not only used in all the classes and lectures, but had to be spoken by the students until after evening prayers ; Latin essays and disputations were required ; public exhibitions of skill in reciting Latin and Greek declensions were given once a week and a recital of the whole grammar, ' especially of the Oxford Latin Grammar ' once a year.

One of the first of these academies was that opened about 1667 by Charles Morton in London (Newington Green (2), see Appendix no. I). It is of special interest seeing that it was there that Daniel Defoe was educated.

Charles Morton, M.A. (Wadham, Oxford), the son of Nicholas Morton, Rector of Blisland (Bodmin), was descended from Cardinal Morton. There are conflicting accounts as to the date when he started his academy, but it was certainly opened after the Five

---

[1] For complete list see Appendix No. I.

[2] ' Our dissenting academies arose out of the universities. Persons educated in the universities afterwards taught what they had there learned and what some of them had there taught.' Bogue and Bennett's *History of Dissenters*, I. p. 296.

Mile Act (prior to 1665 Morton was in Cornwall) and probably not after 1670, for, according to Bogue and Bennett, Morton had an academy nearly 20 years, and it is known that in 1685 he went to New England. Morton was famous for his proficiency in mathematics ; while a student at Oxford his work won the special notice of the Warden, Dr Wilkins, brother-in-law to Cromwell. Morton's qualifications for his position were acknowledged on all sides and under him the academy was most efficient.

Information about this academy is to be obtained from the great Wesley-Palmer controversy. Samuel Wesley (father of John and Charles) first attended Veal's Academy at Stepney, and afterwards, failing to enter at Oxford, went to Newington Green. Wesley afterwards conformed and was untiring in his attacks upon Dissenters. In his ' Letter from a country Divine..on the education of the Dissenters in their private academies in several parts of this nation ' he writes of Morton's Academy, and his account is worth quoting. ' This Academy,' he writes, ' was indeed the most considerable, having annext a fine Garden, Bowling Green, Fish Pond and within, a laboratory and some not inconsiderable rarities with air pump, thermometer, and all sorts of mathematical instruments.' The academy was evidently very much up-to-date. Interesting light is also thrown on the discipline of the academy. After mentioning the names of several persons of quality who were there, he adds, ' and not a few knights' and baronets' sons and one Lord's son, who were sent hither to avoid the debaucheries of the universities, though some of 'em made themselves sufficiently remarkable while they were with us.'

Anxious as Wesley was to condemn the academies whenever possible, he could not say more than this ; and, of course, he practically admits that in the eyes of the public the academies were better, as regards discipline, than the universities. Morton cannot be blamed for the misdemeanours of youths whose parents were afraid to send them to Oxford or Cambridge. According to Wesley, the students themselves were mainly responsible for the discipline. They had, it appears, ' a sort of democratical government ' amongst them, each man being allowed to propose laws and punishments, and to vote (by ballot) their adoption or rejection.

In his ' Defence of the Dissenting Education in their private academies in answer to Mr Wesley's written reflections upon them ' Palmer describes his education under Dr Kerr at Bethnal Green (Period II). He speaks eulogistically of Kerr's treatment of the classical authors and gives a list of studies and books similar to those given in other accounts[1].

It is to Defoe that we owe further details of the subjects and methods in Newington Green. In one of his Reviews Defoe says he had been master of five languages, that he had studied mathematics, natural philosophy, logic, geography, history, and ' politics as a Science.' The last subject, as part of the curriculum of Defoe, whose after life was made up largely of pamphlets and prison as a result of politics ' as an art,' is interesting !

[1] See *The Bethnal Green Course*, p. 62.

In connection with the study of Modern Languages at Morton's Academy, we have still further evidence from Defoe, who, in reply to one Tutchin who had said that Defoe was no scholar, wrote ' As to my little learning and this man's great capacities, I fairly challenge him to translate with me any Latin, French and Italian author, and afterwards to translate them each crossways, for the sum of £20 each book ; and by this he shall have an opportunity to show before the world how much Daniel Defoe, hosier, is inferior to Mr Tutchin, gentleman[1].'

With regard to the method of the academies of his day, the founder of the English novel has a word of censure. ' 'Tis evident that the great imperfection of our academies is the want of conversation. This the public universities enjoy, ours cannot...from our schools we have abundance of instances of men that come away masters of Science, critics in Greek and Hebrew, perfect in languages and perfectly ignorant of their mother tongue[2].' Defoe does record, however, that Morton gave all lectures in English and turned out good preachers.

It is recorded that on one occasion Morton, against whom a ' capias ' was issued, went into concealment, leaving for a short time, a few of his older students in charge—an arrangement which was not in accordance with what Mr Samuel Wesley thought the circumstances required, and consequently that gentleman left 'and did not feel under obligation to refund the Gale exhibition

[1] Wilson's *Life and Times of Defoe*, I. pp. 31, 33.
[2] Wilson, *ibid.*

of £10[1]. This is of interest, not on account of Mr Samuel Wesley's action, but because it throws light on the plans of a benefactor of Dissenters, Theophilus Gale, M.A., the tutor of the other academy at Newington Green (N. G. (1)). By his will most of his property (his library, except philosophical books, went to Harvard) was put in trust to furnish exhibitions of £10 each for students designed for the ministry. Gale, believing that before long students trained in academies would be allowed to qualify for degrees at Oxford and Cambridge, wished each exhibitioner to enter his name at some college so as to be ready to go into residence when the subscribed oaths were no longer required.

From these accounts it will be seen that under Morton Newington Green (2) was an important academy of the first period. There is no doubt that in spite of interruption owing to persecution—seizure of goods and danger of imprisonment—Morton did a good work until, in 1685, he went to New England. There he became pastor of a church, and was chosen Vice-President of Harvard College, where he introduced the systems of science that he used in England. This suggests an interesting field for research ; for it was not through Morton alone that the Dissenting Academies influenced the education of New England. After Morton's departure, three men, Lobb, Wickens (Emmanuel, Cambridge, an authority on Jewish and Oriental subjects), and Glasscock read lectures in the academy, which was discontinued about 1706. This academy is especially noteworthy as exhibiting two features. First, instruction was given which was beyond the grammar

---

[1] *Congregational Historical Soc. Trans.* Vol. III. p. 398.

school standard ; Defoe mentions not only the grammar school subject, Latin, but also Greek, Hebrew, Logic, Mathematics and Science—that is to say, the subjects of the quadrivium, university subjects, were taught. Secondly, many subjects quite outside the ordinary university course were taken, *e.g.* French, Italian, Geography, History. Wesley moreover makes special mention of mathematical (*i.e.* scientific) instruments so that experimental work, though on a small scale, was attempted. Newington Green (2) was no doubt as Wesley said ' the most considerable academy,' and it would be quite wrong to suppose that advanced work of this kind was carried on elsewhere ; but as indicating the development of academical teaching it is important.

Of the other first period London academies we have not such complete accounts. Newington Green (1), famous on account of having given Dr Watts part of his education, and Islington (2) illustrate the necessity the tutors were under of constantly seeking new quarters to avoid the enforcement of the Five Mile Act. Wapping (or Stepney) and Islington (1) died with their founders. The present school at Mill Hill rejoices in being able to trace—along somewhat devious paths, it is true—its descent from the academy set up there about the end of the 17th century.

Details are lacking of the majority of the academies outside London. Many are merely names and are only casually referred to in accounts which noncon-formist historians give of the ejected ministers. There were three, however, which were really noteworthy—Rathmell, Sheriffhales and Shrewsbury.

Rathmell, a little village near Settle, Yorkshire,

has the honour of being ' the oldest Non-conformist seat of learning in the north of England[1].' It was here that Richard Frankland, M.A. (Christ's College, Cambridge), started his famous academy, which was carried on, in spite of much persecution and many removals, for nearly 30 years.

Richard Frankland (born 1630) was educated at Giggleswick Grammar School. (Rathmell is, strictly speaking, a hamlet in the parish of Giggleswick.) Later, he was sent to Cambridge where he took B.A. 1651 and M.A. 1655. He was afterwards appointed to a living at Bishop Auckland, and when Cromwell was making arrangements for the university which he proposed to establish at Durham, Frankland was mentioned in connection with a Tutorship[2]. Owing to the Restoration, of course, that College was never started. In 1661 Frankland lost his living. After being ejected from Bishop Auckland he went to Rathmell, near his old home, and a little later, acting upon the suggestion of his friends, he began an academy there. The first pupil was George Liddell, the son of Frankland's friend, Sir Thos. Liddell, who entered March 8th, 1669. In four years he received 15 pupils, six of whom became nonconformist ministers. He then removed to Natland near Kendal, and during the nine years of his stay there he not only continued his work as a minister and preacher, but instructed 77 students. Kendal was a corporate town, and at length the Five Mile Act was enforced and Frankland removed to Calton-in-Craven near Settle. Though some pupils went with him, there

---

[1] *Congregational Historical Soc. Trans.* Vol. II. p. 422.
[2] There seems to be no evidence of his appointment.

is no doubt that this removal and the three which followed in the next three years—first to Dawsonfield (near Crosthwaite), second to Hullbarrow (near Cartmell Fell) and then to Attercliffe—interrupted his work very seriously, and yet, in spite of this, his fame seems to have been spreading ; for, during the period 1686–1699 no fewer than 51 students were received. After the Revolution and the Toleration Act, Rathmell again became the seat of the academy, which continued there till a few months after Frankland's death. During this last period about 142 students were trained, some for the ministry (about one-third of the total number became ministers) and some for the other professions. The entire number of Frankland's students is given as 303. There is no doubt that this was certainly the most important academy in the north of England, and that it reached so eminent a position, in spite of disturbance which would have gone far to destroy many institutions, is a high tribute to Frankland and his work.

In his *Life of Rev. John Ashe*[1], James Clegg, M.D. (himself a student under Frankland, and Ashe's nephew), says that in 1688 Ashe went under " That well-known tutor Rev. Mr Frankland who had then under his conduct the most numerous and flourishing private academy in England and who was indeed by great learning, wisdom and an admirable temper excellently qualified for that Post and service...I never knew a tutor so entirely beloved by them all nor one that so well deserved it. His unaffected gravity, sweetened with candour, meekness and humility,

---

[1] *Life of Rev. John Ashe*, p. 53.

procured him that esteem and veneration even from the most licentious, that made them ever afraid of grieving or offending him.'

Nor was it the students only who esteemed him ; he won the goodwill of every one who was privileged to know him and counted among his friends, not only many Dissenters, but several Anglicans also, among whom was Archbishop Sharp, a friend who later rendered Frankland good service. Frankland was one of the tutors who were persecuted on the pretence of having broken the ' Oxford Oath[1].' For centuries all Oxford and Cambridge graduates had been required to swear that they would not teach ' as in a University ' without the sanction of the university authorities—an oath which had remained long after the reason for it (the attempted new university at Stamford, 1334) had vanished, and an oath moreover, to which no one attached any importance whatever. It was used, however, as a pretext for persecuting many tutors in dissenting academies. On one occasion

---

[1] Every graduate swears :

(1) To keep and observe the statutes, privileges, customs and liberties of the University.

(2) You shall also swear that in that Faculty to which you are now admitted Graduate, you shall not solemnly perform your readings as in a University anywhere within this kingdom but here in Oxford or in Cambridge ; nor shall you take degrees, as in a University, in any Faculty whatsoever, nor shall you consent that any person who hath taken his Degree elsewhere shall be admitted as a master here in the said Faculty, to which he shall be elsewhere admitted.

(3) You shall also swear that you will not read lectures, or hear them read, at Stamford, as in a University study, or college general.

Frankland was ordered to appear before the bishop's court and on his not appearing he was excommunicated. His friends, however, Lord Wharton and Sir Thomas Rokeby, took up the matter, and as a result, William III ordered his absolution to be read in Giggleswick Church. Later, in 1697, proceedings against him, in an ecclesiastical court, were stopped, it is believed, by Archbishop Sharp's intervention.

To Rathmell, in 1695, was sent James Clegg, who writes thus: ' I was sent to Frankland's at Rathmell, a noted Academy in the North. He had at that time about eighty young men (who boarded with him and in the town near him) to whom he read Lectures with the help of an assistant.' This assistant was probably Mr Issot, an old pupil ; there are mentioned also two other pupils as assistants, Richard Frankland the younger and John Owen, but whether they were Frankland's colleagues is not definitely known—so large a number as 80 students, however, would make it imperative that there should be at least one other tutor.

Clegg reproaches himself for not applying himself more earnestly to his work and for being too ready to read the ' light ' English books read by Frankland's daughters. The diary contains no account of the work done during Clegg's time, but in the *Life of Rev. John Ashe* (p. 55), Clegg tells us of the work his uncle did. A rough time-table, drawn up from this account, is given on p. 68. No doubt the work was very similar in Clegg's own time.

In 1698 Clegg records ' In October the great and good old man Mr Frankland died. I saw him depart.

This was a wide breach ; now we were left as sheep without a shepherd. Mr Chorlton was desired to take charge of the academy but declined it. Afterwards others were proposed, but none were fully agreed upon and the young men began to drop away and so that academy fell.'

After Frankland's death, very determined efforts were made to continue the academy which had been doing such admirable work and which was, of course, a means of supplying the pulpits in the north of England. Oliver Heywood several times refers to the difficulty of getting any one to fill Frankland's post, and at last, as Clegg says, the students began to leave. Heywood gives a list of several who went to Manchester, and among these was Clegg who records this removal in his diary—' In 1699,' he says, ' when I left Rathmell, I placed myself in Manchester for the benefit of the library and the conversation of other young

Frankland's Academy. (Clegg's *Ashe.*)

7 a.m.	Prayers.			
	Breakfast.			
9 (?)	Lectures	Logic, Metaphysics, Somatology, Pneumatology, Natural Philosophy.	*Thursdays*	Theses and public Disputations appointed by Tutor.
			Saturdays, 5–6	(before evening prayer) Analysis, *i.e.* methodical and critical dissertation on some verses of psalm or chapter.
12 (?)	Dinner.			
	Private reading or Recreation.			
6 p.m.	Prayers.			
	Supper.			
	Students' Discussion in own rooms.			

scholars.... Several young men who had been under Mr Frankland's tuition also came about that time and placed themselves under Mr Chorlton.'

With Frankland's death, therefore, Rathmell ceased to be the seat of the great Northern Academy, but, as Clegg and Oliver Heywood record, eleven of Frankland's students finished their course under Chorlton who ' set up teaching University learning in a great house in Manchester.' Chorlton's Academy is therefore looked upon as the successor to Rathmell. As at Newington Green (2) so at Rathmell, the work was of university standard. It is interesting to note that only a third of the large number of students entered the ministry. There must have been a great demand for the new ' realistic ' instruction ; for Rathmell, it must be remembered, was but *one* of 22 academies known to have been founded by ejected ministers. It is true that the majority were quite small, but the following accounts will show that even in the small academies important work was being done. A fairly full account of the academy at Sheriffhales (Shropshire) under the Rev. John Woodhouse, is given by Toulmin[1], who obtained his information from MSS. lent to him by Mr John Woodhouse Crompton of Birmingham.

The Sheriffhales Academy was in existence from 1663–1697. Here the students were trained for the various professions, and, as was usual, took a course of lectures in logic, anatomy, mathematics, physics, ethics, and rhetoric—these all the students took

[1] Toulmin, *Historical View of the State of the Protestant Dissenters in England*, Vol. II. p. 225.

and then, later, specialised in Theology, Law or Medicine[1].

From the records which we have of the method employed, it would seem that Mr Woodhouse was very careful to require thorough work. Lectures were not merely delivered, with no thought as to whether they were understood or remembered. Careful explanation was given and, before a new lecture started, an account of the preceding one was required, and the lectures were ' commonly committed to memory, at least as to the sense of them.'

Sheriffhales is noticeable as a first period academy in which work outside the ordinary curriculum was done. Classics, of course, came first, and public declensions and disputations had a prominent place week by week, and especially on the great day of the year, when the whole grammar was recited ; but this

---

[1] *Arts Course at Sheriffhales.*

Authors chiefly studied.

Mathematics	Galtruchius, Gassendi, Gunter, Leybourn, Moxon, and Euclid's *Elements*.
Natural Science	De Carte's *Principia*, De Stair, Heereboord, Magirus, Rhegius, Robault.
Logic	Burgedicius with Heereboord's *Commentary*, Sanderson Wallis, Ramus and his commentator Downam for private study.
Rhetoric	Quintilian, Radeau, Vossius.
Metaphysics	Baronius, Facchaeus, Frommenius ; all Blank's *Theses* and Ward's *Determinationes*.
Ethics	Eustachius, Heereboord, More, Whitby.
Geography	Euchard.
History	Puffendorf.
Anatomy	Gibson, Bartoline and Blancardi, *Anatomia Reformata*.
Hebrew	Bythner's *Grammar* and his *Lyra Prophetica*.

was not all. We are told that ' Practical exercises accompanied the course of lectures and the students were employed at times in surveying land, composing almanacs, making sun dials of different constructions, and dissecting animals '—this reminds one of Milton's recommendations. But even more important than these practical exercises is a statement to the effect that the students were in the habit of writing English compositions in the form of letters and speeches, ' And,' continues the writer, ' students designed for the ministry drew up skeletons or heads of sermons, schemes of prayer, etc., and set psalms to two or three tunes (metres ?).' Whether the writing of English composition may be traced to the influence of the sermon-writing required in the divinity course is not known ; but the hypothesis seems probable, and if there were casual connection between the two, it is not unlikely that the adoption, in the other academies, of English in the lectures (long before it was adopted in Oxford or Cambridge) and later, of English as a subject in itself, is due to the same cause.

Sheriffhales did not become so large as Rathmell, but there is evidence of there having been 40 students in residence at one time, and this accounts for the fact of the names of two ministers, Southwell and Beresford being given (but in sources other than the MSS.) as those of Woodhouse's assistants, though whether they really did occupy that position is not certain.

Among the students were several ministers and lawyers, and also some who filled, if not better, yet more public positions. Among these were Robert Harley, Earl of Oxford and Henry St John, Viscount

Bolingbroke. It was these men who afterwards, in 1714, supported the Schism Bill which enacted that ' no person should keep any public or private school or teach or instruct unless he conforms to the Established Church.' The bill, it will be remembered, passed the Commons with a large majority—owing largely to the strenuous endeavours of Harley. In the Lords, however, it was vigorously opposed, and in a strong speech Lord Wharton, ever ready to uphold Nonconformists, reproached Harley, saying ' Such a measure was but an indifferent return for the benefit which the public had received from these schools in which the greatest men had been educated—men who had made a glorious peace for England, who had paid the debts of the nation, and who had extended its commerce.' Such is the testimony of a contemporary who was well qualified (since he was acquainted with many tutors and schools) to speak of the work of the academies.

But before this, the academy at Sheriffhales had ceased to exist—owing, it is thought, to ill-health, Woodhouse had to leave Shropshire for London, and in consequence, in 1697, the academy was closed.

Two years later, however, another academy in the same county was becoming important.

The chief source of information about this academy, which was situated at Shrewsbury, is the MS. in Dr Williams's Library. Soon after the ejection, an academy was started in Shrewsbury by Francis Tallents, M.A. (Cambridge) Fellow and then Vice-President of Magdalen College, who, in 1642, was in France as tutor to the Earl of Suffolk's sons. Tallents ministered to the Nonconformists in Shrewsbury, as also did Bryan, and the two were associated in academical teaching. It was not, however, until the academy came under the control of James Owen in 1699, that it became very strong.   Owen had started an academy in Oswestry about 1660.   He was, according to the MS. ' versed in many languages ancient and modern, but his greatest skill was in history, especially ecclesiastical.'   The account also says ' As to polemical Divinity, he was a champion.'   No doubt Owen's powers in this direction would have some influence on the pupils and though there is no mention of English as a subject, it may be conjectured that, as in other academies, it was given some slight notice.   The following list of authors read at Shrewsbury is taken from the MS. (Dr Williams's Library) :

Logic	.. ..	Burgersdicius, Heereboord, Ramus.
Metaphysics	..	Frommenius, Eustachius, Baronius.
Philosophy	..	Le Clerc, Du Hamel.
Geometry	..	Euclid, Pardie (??).
Astronomy	..	Gassendius.
Chronology	..	Strauchius.
Ecclesiastical ⎱ History ⎰	..	Spanheim.
Theology..	..	Wollebius, Byssemus.

Among the list of students at Shrewsbury during Owen's time are the names of two who afterwards occupied important positions as tutors—Perrot of Carmarthen 1715–1733 and Samuel Jones of Tewkesbury.

James Owen died 1706 and his place was filled by Samuel Benion, M.D., who, after 1691, was with Philip Henry at Broad Oak.   Here Benion seems to have taught some youths boarding with Henry and to have received instruction from him in ' Academical Knowledge ' and in theological studies. It is recorded of Benion that at Shrewsbury ' he hit upon a better plan of education than his predecessors. He drew up several schemes of sciences, logic, pneumatology, natural philosophy, ethics '—but here the manuscript stops, leaving us ignorant of the exact nature of the changes.

The academy continued under Reynolds and Giles until about 1708, when many of the students left, to attend either Jones' Academy at Tewkesbury or Latham's at Findern, which were then growing and becoming more important.

Such, then were the academies of the first period. As we have seen, they resembled the grammar schools ; but the best of them worked more and more on university lines. There is no doubt that classics had the chief place in the curriculum, then came logic, rhetoric, mathematics, theology and law—in these subjects lectures were read by the tutor. The lectures seem to have been designed to throw light upon the text-book—that is, the text-book was the basis of the lectures, which were not given independently of any one book. Before a new lecture, questions were often asked to ascertain what the students remembered of the previous one, and after the lecture they were allowed to ask for further explanations if necessary. Besides the set text-books there were books recommended for private reading. The text-books were those ordinarily used by university students. Henry Fleming, an undergraduate at Queen's College, Oxford, who went up in 1678, read the same books that were used at Sheriffhales and Shrewsbury. In logic, Brerewood,

Sanderson and Burgersdicius, in ethics, Eustachius, Brerewood[1]. An interesting difference is that both the Sheriffhales and the Shrewsbury list mention the logic by Ramus—this, apparently, was not known to Fleming. As a rule in the early academies there were no *lectures* in Geography, History, Natural philosophy, Anatomy, Ethics, and Metaphysics; books on these subjects were read privately and occasionally the students' work was ' heard.' The only one of these subjects which seems to have interested Henry Fleming was Geography ; his letters to his father contain requests for a geography book and his accounts show he possessed one and an atlas, but there is strong reason for thinking that this was an interest outside his university course and akin to the half-amused interest which his father and his tutor took in the early beginnings of the Ashmolean Museum or the ' knick-knackery ' as it was called.

The above account of academy work would in all probability apply to all the academies of the first period—that is to say if details of the work in all of them were available it would be unlikely that one would be found doing less than this ; there were, however, some in which, as has been seen, even more advanced work was taken—English essays, at Sheriffhales ; modern languages, at Newington Green ; practical exercises in science, at both these places ; such work, however, in the first period was exceptional ; it was not until the later years of the second period that the majority of the academies undertook it.

The second period academies (1691–1750) were more ' public ' than the early ones. In some cases

[1] See *The Flemings in Oxford*, Vol. I. pp. 250–255, 321.

they had been private academies which, after the death of the founder or the early tutors, were controlled by a group of ministers who had the appointment of the tutor in their hands—the appointment of P. Doddridge as the successor of Jennings of Kibworth is a case in point ; in other cases they were founded as the result of the efforts of leading Dissenters and were supported by the churches, by ministers' societies or by such funds as that of the London Congregational Fund Board (1695). They were therefore not the property of the tutor (as those started by the ejected ministers had been) and were under some measure of ' public ' control. These academies differ chiefly from those of the first period just described in being not only more ' public ' but also in having several tutors each of whom was a specialist in his subject, with the result that one academy became the resort of those reading theology, another, of those reading mathematics, and a third of those requiring science, and so, as in the earlier days, students travelled from academy to academy[1]. Moreover, the academies of this period, while teaching university subjects and employing university methods, yet became more and more modern. Classics still remained important, but Latin had to be spoken only at certain times and in certain places. Before the end of this period all lectures were, not as formerly, in Latin, but in English. English exercises and essays were required and even English books, *e.g.* Bacon's Essays at Kibworth, were read ; that is to say, English

---

[1] Secker went from Attercliffe to Tewkesbury (probably for Theology) and thence to London (No. 22, period II) to study Science under J. Eames, F.R.S.

was read as literature—not because it was a vehicle of information. The second period academies are of great interest seeing that they illustrate very clearly on the one hand the growing demand for a ' realistic education ' and on the other hand the desire on the part of the academies to adapt their work to the needs of the day. Thirty-four academies are grouped in the second period ; among them are several which have been continued as theological training colleges—Attercliffe is connected through the old Rotherham College with the present Yorkshire United College, Bradford—Idle and Heck-mondwyke are also connected with the same institution : practically no records were kept of the actual teaching in the majority of the academies ; but we are fortunate in having a full account from various sources of the work of Northampton Academy, which from the influence it exerted was by far the most important in this period. Under the Rev. Philip Doddridge, D.D., the academy at Northampton became one of the most famous in the country. It was in reality a continuation of an academy to which Doddridge himself had gone in 1719 when a youth of seventeen, and which was started at Kibworth in Leicestershire about 1715 by the Rev. John Jennings.

In a letter[1] (dated 1728) to the Rev. Thomas Saunders, Doddridge gives a very full account of his education under Jennings. The course, so far as classics and theology are concerned, is similar to that in the academies of the first period, but far more time was given to modern subjects. Doddridge writes ' Our

[1] *Correspondence and diary of P. Doddridge* (ed. by Humphreys), Vol. II. p. 462.

course of education at Kibworth was the employment
of four years and every half year we entered upon a
new set of studies or at least changed the time and
order of our lectures.' The first half year's work was
as follows—' Geometry and algebra, three times a week
[*i.e.* the work of the ' quadrivium ' was started], Hebrew
twice, Geography, French, Latin prose authors and
classical exercises once a week.' Boyer's French
Grammar was used and there was some reading of
phrases and dialogues ' without regarding the pronunciation with which Mr Jennings was not acquainted.'
It will be noticed that a lecture period was given to
geography. ' The lecture,' writes Doddridge, ' was
only an examination of the account we could give of
the most remarkable passages ' of Gordon's Geography ;
this comment also applies to history taken in the second
half year. Reference to the full course[1] will show not
only when the usual subjects such as Divinity, Jewish
Antiquities, Ecclesiastical history, Pneumatology, etc.
were taken, but also that science, mechanics, hydrostatics, physics, anatomy, and astronomy had an important place in the time-table ; that English essays,
with Bacon, Addison and Steele as models, were
regularly written ; and that in the oratory class
' English orations were the most common and turned,
I believe, to the best account.'

After giving all the work and the text-books used
Doddridge gives some information about the general
administration of the academy. All the students were
examined before admission and were expected to have
done some Latin. The students had always to converse

[1] See Appendix No. II.

in Latin at certain times and in certain places ; the scriptures were read ' in the family ' (*i.e.*, when they all assembled for prayers) from Hebrew, Greek, or French into English.   Mr Jennings allowed the students to use his library.   In summer they rose at 6.30, in winter at 7.30 ; they had a fortnight's vacation at Christmas and six weeks at Whitsuntide.   An idea of the fees will be gained from Doddridge's bill at Christmas, 1720 :

	£	s.	d.
Half year's board and tuition ..	8	10	0
King's ' Inquiry '		4	3
Appendix to Logic		2	6
Interleaved New Testament ..		3	8
	£9	0	5

In 1722 the academy removed to Hinkley.   Mr Jennings died in 1723, and it was some time before a successor was appointed.   At last, at a general meeting of Nonconformist ministers, held at Lutterworth, April 1729, it was suggested that the academy should be established at Harborough [1] and Dr Doddridge began his work there in the following June [2].   Before his appointment, Doddridge had some correspondence on the matter with several ministers, among whom was Dr Isaac Watts, whose letters throw light on the work and position of academies in those days.   For example, in one of his letters Watts says ' You will have many lads coming from the Grammar Schools, and as many such scholars will not be fit to enter upon your academical course with proper advantage, should

---

[1] The removal to Northampton was made in the same year—1729.

[2] This shows the more ' public' character of the IInd period academies.

not the perfection of the studies of grammar, algebra and geometry be the business of your first half year[1] ? " Doddridge replies ' I propose that the perfection of these studies should be the employment of the first year.' Again, Dr Watts says ' Are the hands of the enemies effectually chained up from offering us any violence, that they cannot indict or persecute you under the pretence that your academy is a school ? ' Doddridge replies ' I know not how it may be in other places, but about us I cannot discern so much fury in the clergy ; nor do I imagine they could make anything of a prosecution. It was once attempted, to the shame of the undertakers, with regard to Mr Matchens of Mount Sorrel[2].'

As a matter of fact, however, the clergy did attempt a prosecution. No sooner had the academy begun to thrive than attempts were made to injure it. The Archdeacon of Northampton, Dr Reynolds, ordered the wardens of All Saints to ' present ' the ' fellow in the parish who taught a Grammar School ' unless he held a proper licence from the Bishop. The citation is still preserved and is given in the *History of Castle Hill Church*[3]. It is worth giving in full.

To Philip Dotteridge of the Parish of All Saints, in the Town of Northampton, in the County of Northampton, Gentleman.

By virtue of a Citation under seal herewith shewn unto you I cite you to appear personally before the Reverend George Reynolds Doctor of laws Vicar General Commissary General

---

[1] *Diary and Correspondence of P. Doddridge* (ed. Humphreys), Vol. II. p. 478 *et seq.*

[2] *Ibid.* Vol. II. p. 481.   [3] p. 21.

and Official Principal in spiritual matters of the Right Reverend father in God Robert by Divine Permission Lord Bishop of Peterborough and also official of the Reverend the Archdeacon of the Archdeaconry of Northampton or his lawfull Surrogate or some other competent Judge in this behalfe in the Consistory Court adjoyning to the Parish Church of All Saints in the same town of Northampton on Tuesday the sixth day of November 1733 at the usual time of hearing causes there then and there to answer to certain Articles or Interrogations to be objected and administered to you concerning your soul's health and the Reformation and correction of your manners and excess. And especially your teaching and instructing youth in the Liberal Arts and Sciences not being licensed thereto by the Ordinary of the Diocese touching either your Learning and Dexterity in teaching or your right understanding of God's true religion or your honest and sober conversation at the promotion of and pursuant to a certain Detection or present ment exhibited against you by Thomas Rand and Benjamin Chapman, Churchwardens of the said parish of All Saints in the said town of Northampton. And farther to do and receive according to Law—Justice.

W. M. Spencer.

' Doddridge was promised a licence if he would apply, but fortified with the assistance of the London Committee of Protestant Dissenters he refused.'

Doddridge appealed against the Citation and finally, nearly a year afterwards, the whole proceedings were stopped by a message from George II, who insisted ' that in his reign there should be no persecution for conscience' sake[1].'

Doddridge began with only three pupils intended for the ministry and says of them ' they had made a very considerable progress, both in Latin and Greek ; indeed, far beyond what many others have done who

[1] *History of Castle Hill Church*, pp. 21 and 22.

have just left a Grammar School.' In 1732, David Jennings wrote to Doddridge, strongly advising him to change his intention of taking only students who meant to be ministers. Jennings thought it a mistake to compel Dissenters to send their sons who were to be physicians, lawyers or gentlemen to Oxford or Cambridge, or ' to make them rakes in foreign universities.' Doddridge needed no second advice, but at once threw open his academy to boys preparing for the various professions, and consequently his numbers increased. The average number in residence was, probably, between 30 and 50. In 1730 there were about 40 ; in 1743 63 signed the rules Doddridge drew up ; in 1747 there were only 29. A letter[1] to the Rev. John Barker, who had written about a poor youth of exceptional promise, shows Doddridge ready to take the boy, though he does not generally take boys who have not been through a grammar school and acquired a good knowledge of classics. The fees were £16 per annum, for board (students dependent on charity funds, *i.e.*, collections from churches, paid £14 per annum for board) and £4 for tuition. When pupils enter the academy, says Doddridge, ' they pay a guinea each for a closet and bring a pair of sheets. They find their own candles and put out their washing.' A comparison between these terms at Northampton and Doddridge's Kibworth bill given above (p. 79) with the following sent home by Pitt, Earl of Chatham, who was at Oxford during the same period, serves to illustrate the

---

[1] *Correspondence and Diary of P. Doddridge* (ed. Humphreys), Vol. III. p. 206.

enormous expense which was avoided by sending youths to an academy.

TRINITY COLLEGE,
January ye 20th, 1726/7.

HOND. SIR.

After such delay, tho' not owing to any negligence on my part, I am ashamed to send you ye following accompt without first making great apologies for not executing your commands sooner.

	£	s.	d.
Matriculation Fees		16	6
Caution Money	10	0	0
Benefaction	10	0	0
Utensils for ye Coll.	2	0	0
Common Room	2	0	0
Coll.-servants' fees	1	15	0
Poddesway gown & cap	8	12	0
Tea table china ware, etc. ..	6	5	0
Glasses		11	0
Thirds of chamber & furniture ..	41	7	8
Teaspoons	1	7	6
Summe total	84	14	8
Balance paid me by Mr Stockwell	15	05	4

I have too much reason to fear you may think some of these articles too extravagant, as they really are, but all I have to say for it is, humbly to beg you would not attribute it to my extravagance but to ye custom of this place, where we pay for most things too at a high rate...and am with all possible respect

Sr. Yr. most dutyfull son

WM. PITT.

Moreover, three months later, April 10th[1], Pitt sent home another bill for £47. 5s. 0d. which includes the following items : ' Three months' learning French

---

[1] *Chatham,* Rosebery, p. 34.

£2. 2s. 0d.; for a course of experimental philosophy
£2. 2s. 0d.' and at Northampton the terms were £4 for
tuition per annum—with French and experimental
philosophy included ! It is not surprising in view of
these facts that ' it frequently happened that the
clergy and lay members of the National Church to
whom the expense of the University was an object of
difficulty availed themselves of these academies with
advantage and without any fear that an undue influence
would be exercised upon the minds of the children[1].'
A letter which Dr Doddridge received from Lord
Kilkerran (Sir James Fergusson) in 1743 gives another
reason for the growing popularity of the academies.
Lord Kilkerran says ' the education of my children in
a right way is what I have much at heart and that
I foresee many dangers in sending them to the University, I have been of opinion that the better way is
to send them to an academy under virtuous people.'

From the first, discipline in the academies had
received the careful attention of the tutors and reference
is often found to regulations framed to secure good order
and strict attention to work. Probably the most
detailed rules for an academy were drawn up by
Doddridge in 1643[2]. There were several sections dealing with such matters as ' Attendance on Family
Prayer and Lectures at appointed times ' ; ' Of shutting
up the gate and retiring to bed ' ; ' Of the Hours, Place
and Order of Meals.' There is a section containing
the usual Library rules and one with regulations for

[1] Quoted from J. D. Humphreys, editor of the *Diary and Correspondence of Dr Doddridge*, Vol. I. p. 31.

[2] A *History of Castle Hill Church, Northampton,* contains a copy
of the original manuscript book now at New College, London.

' Conduct when Abroad,' *i.e.* when outside the academy. A selection of these rules is given in Appendix No. III. Perhaps the most important here is Section II, No. 3, which requires every student to be ready for lecture within five minutes of the hour fixed or to forfeit twopence ; this rule was meant to be obeyed, for in the section dealing with the duties of the office of the monitor we find that he had to call over the roll not only before morning and evening prayer but also before ' all lectures appointed for the whole academy together and if he fail to do it—he is to forfeit sixpence for every such failure.' The usual fines were required for being ' Gated ' and a further regulation reads ' when the small pecuniary fines here appointed evidently appear to be despised, they will be exchanged for some extraordinary exercises, which, if they are not performed, must occasion complaint to the friends of the student in question ; for the intent of these laws is not to enrich the box at the expense of those who are determined to continue irregular but to prevent any from being so.' A rule requiring tradesmen's bills to be delivered to the Tutor twice a year when all accounts had to be settled would probably do much to prevent the extravagant running up of bills which was so often a source of trouble to parents whose sons were at Oxford or Cambridge. The section dealing with ' Academical studies ' will be better taken when the course of instruction is under consideration. That claims attention now.

The time-table and course of lectures may be tabulated as follows :

Northampton Academy Time-table.

a.m.		p.m.	
6.	Rise	2.	Dinner.
6.10.	Roll-call and prayers. Private reading.	7.	Evening prayers. 'Tutorials' or "coaching" in languages.
8.	Family Prayer. Breakfast.	before 9.	Supper.
10–2 p.m.	Lectures.	10.	Gate locked.
		10.30.	Students in their own rooms.

Lectures from 10 a.m.—2 p.m.

First Year	Second Year	Third Year	Fourth Year
Logic	Trigonometry	Natural ⎫ History	Civil Law
Rhetoric	Conic Sections	Civil ⎭	Mythology
Geography	Celestial	Anatomy	and Hiero-
Metaphysics	Mechanics	Jewish Antiquities	glyphics
Geometry	Natural and	Divinity	English Hist.
Algebra	Experimental	Orations	Hist. of Non-
	Philosophy		conformity
	Divinity		Divinity
	Orations		Preaching
			Pastoral
			Care, etc.

It will be seen that in the first year Logic and Rhetoric, the two subjects of the trivium, ignored in the grammar schools, were taken together with the ' first steps ' in the quadrivium—Geography, Geometry and Algebra. The second year's work was devoted mainly to the quadrivium, and from Orton's *Life of Doddridge* we learn that the system of natural and experimental philosophy (comprehending mechanics, statics, hydrostatics, optics, pneumatology, and astronomy) was read ' with reference to the best authors on these subjects and was illustrated by a neat and pretty large philosophical apparatus.' This natural and experimental philosophy did not contain anything very advanced, and the method was probably either that the tutor read to the students his own ' system ' (lectures) consisting of information gleaned from such books as then existed on the subject, or that the students read the chief books, and the lecture consisted in ' hearing ' their account of the chief parts. But though the lectures were no doubt superficial, yet the fact, which must not be lost sight of, is that such subjects were taken and that an attempt, however crude, was made to take them experimentally. In the third and fourth years history has a notable place and more time was given to specialisation ; naturally the students wishing to qualify as lawyers or doctors would not be required to attend lectures on Divinity and Preaching ; for them special lectures were given in required subjects so as to fit them to take up more advanced reading in such institutions as were specially concerned with the training for the medical and legal professions. The arrangement of the course is quite on university lines and quite in accordance with the suggestion of Milton who, it will be remembered, considered that at an academy a good general and useful education should be given in all subjects and that highly specialised work was to be taken in separate institutions.

One important omission from the time-table claims our attention. Languages are conspicuous by their absence—except that there were evening tutorials in languages, and that at prayers the students read the Bible from Hebrew, Greek, Latin, or French into

English. This seems to suggest that languages were neglected ; in fact Priestley, who went as a student to the academy the year after Doddridge's death, 1751 (when probably Doddridge's methods were continued), speaks of getting up early to do Greek with another student, and adds ' These voluntary engagements were the more necessary in the course of our academical studies as there was then no provision made for teaching the learned languages. We had even no compositions or orations in Latin[1].' Doddridge was evidently no Ciceronian, but there is considerable evidence to show that languages were not ignored. In 1750, Dr Doddridge wrote that he hoped to have a third tutor ' who, while I am employed in theological studies, and Mr Clark in philosophy, might teach the languages not only to academical pupils but also to some lads who are forming their first acquaintance with them, or who... .are not of an age, standing or attainments to be ranked with any of our classes.' This suggests that Doddridge was, at this time, not requiring from students on entrance even a good grounding in Latin and Greek, and it suggests, too, either (1) that he was taking in younger boys than he did at first—taking them before they had really finished at the grammar school or (2) if they were boys of the usual age, 16 or 17, that they were not so well prepared by the grammar school as they had been 10 or 11 years before. But from a statement by Bogue and Bennett[2] it seems that Doddridge from the first gave help to backward students after evening prayers in Latin, Greek, and

---

[1] *Life and Correspondence of Joseph Priestley*, Rutt, II. p. 26.
[2] *History of Dissenters*, Vol. II. p. 334.

Hebrew, so that he was really engaging a third tutor not to do new work but to relieve him of work which had always had a place on the time-table. Indeed, in the rules drawn up by Doddridge (see Appendix No. III) No. 10 in Section I dealing with academical studies provides for definite ' private ' reading in classics for all students. The rule is ' four classics, viz. one Greek and one Latin poet and one Greek and one Latin prose writer, as appointed by the tutor, are to be read by each student in his study and observations are to be written upon them to be kept in a distinct book, and communicated to the tutor whenever he shall think fit.' This provision and the fact that language classes were of the nature of ' tutorials '—coaching students with special needs—indicate that Doddridge in the true realistic spirit condemned excessive study of languages and did not require more than a general knowledge from a student unless he was preparing for some profession in which specialised knowledge was required[1]. For example, Lord Kilkerran writing in 1743 about his son, said he was 17 and had learnt Latin and Greek at a public school, but that as he was intending to study Law he would require to do more Latin. The rules, already referred to, show that in the first and second years a Latin disputation alternated with an English one ; if Latin compositions or orations were not required in Priestley's day (1752–1755) the probability is that

[1] The MS. account (Dr Williams's Library) of Tutors and Academies gives the course at Daventry (whither the Northampton Academy removed after the death of Doddridge) and adds this note ' The French lang. is taught when desired & ev. student designed for a learned profession takes his turn in orations and other public exercises.'

before his death (1752) Doddridge had become still more firmly convinced of the wisdom of requiring all essays to be in English.

The rules for ' Academical Studies ' are important and are here given in full.   They show the care with which the work was arranged and the steps taken to see that requirements were fulfilled.   Doddridge had a keen sense not only of the value of education but of the greatness of the responsibility of his position.

Section I.   Of Academical Studies.

1.   *1st year*.   Translations from Latin into English and vice versa as appointed by the tutors to be showed them at the day and hour appointed and in the last three months of the year orations are to be exhibited in Latin and English alternately every Thursday, which is also to be the time of the following exercises.

2.   In first half of second year these orations are to be continued, and in the latter part of the year each is in his turn to exhibit a Philosophical Thesis or Dissertation.

3.   In third year Ethical Theses or Dissertations are to be exhibited weekly as above, and toward the end of this year and during the fourth Theological.

4.   The Revolution of these is to be so adjusted that every student may compose at least six orations, Theses or Dissertations before the conclusion of his fourth year.

5.   .   .   .   .   .   .

6.   .   .   .   .   .   .

7. Exercises are to be first written in a paper book, then reviewed and corrected by one of the tutors, after that, fairly transcribed, and after they have been exhibited in the manner which shall be appointed, a fair copy of them, with the author's name annexed, shall be delivered to the tutor.

8. Two sermons on given subjects to be composed by every theological student in his eighth year, to be read over by him in the class, and having been there corrected to be preached in the family if the student does not propose preaching in public before he leave the Academy, and besides these, at least six schemes of other sermons on given texts are to be exhibited in the class during the fourth year by each student.

10. Four classics, viz. one Greek and one Latin poet and one Greek and one Latin prose writer as appointed by the tutor are to be read by each student in his study and observations are to be written upon them, to be kept in a distinct book, and communicated to the tutor whenever he shall think fit.

11. Each student of the upper class may be allowed to propose a difficult scripture to the Principal Tutor every Thursday to be discussed by him the next Thursday. But it will be expected that the person proposing them write some memorandum of the solution...etc.

12. ...each Theological Pupil will be expected to write, either at meeting or afterward....Hints of all the Sermons he hears, to be examined by the Tutor ...etc.

13. On the four Thursdays preceding the long vacation, the whole Academy is to meet at ten in the

morning. and all the forenoon is to be spent in the examination of Students....And on the first of these days disputations shall be held by the two upper classes in the Presence of the Juniors, that they may learn by example the method of Disputation...etc.

14. In case of a total neglect of preparing an appointed exercise sixpence is to be forfeited to the box....

The chief part of Doddridge's teaching was with the theological students ; the staple of their curriculum was a ' system ' of two hundred and fifty lectures (the preparation of which occupied many years of Doddridge's life) on ' The Principal subjects in Pneumatology (*i.e.* Psychology), Ethics and Divinity.' These lectures were in English and were followed by questions and discussions about any points not perfectly clear. Jennings, Doddridge's predecessor, had always lectured in Latin, as did most of the tutors of the period, but so great was the influence of Doddridge that his lectures in English were imitated with the result that after his day a lecture in Latin (in an academy) was exceptional. Before a new lecture Doddridge generally questioned the students on what had been taken at the last ; during the lecture (and during sermons, too) the students were required to take notes in shorthand and to transcribe as much as possible afterwards. Rich's shorthand as improved by Doddridge was, therefore, studied.

Doddridge's students came from all parts of the United Kingdom and some even from Holland ; among them were several who occupied positions of importance as lawyers, doctors or ministers in various parts of the country. One of these ministers was Samuel

Mercer[1] of Chowbent, Lancashire ; in his *Lancashire Nonconformity*[2] Mr Nightingale gives a letter from young Samuel Mercer while at the academy, to his parents. It is well worth giving in full.

Novr. 12, 1750.

HONOURED PARENTS,

" I received your last, which I had intended to have answered sooner, had I not had so much business upon my hands, which to have omitted would have been to my disadvantage, etc. As for seeing you and my brother at Northampton I should be extremely glad, but, perhaps, you may think that may be an excuse for my not coming home, for, I will assure you that I cannot go to London along with you, for our vacation will begin the latter end of June, so that if you come it will be unnecessary charges for you to come through Northampton, but I should be very glad if you would send me word in your next letter whether you would have me come home or no, etc.

" If I have been extravagant in my expenses I am not sensible of it. You see always all my bills that are of any importance, and as I have sent you some enclosed in this letter, which I hope you will have no objection to. The everlasting which you see is for two pair of.........waistcoats, one pair of which I have worn out almost ; and my gown is so far gone that it will scarce last me till a few weeks longer. I have bought a new wig which I stood in great need of. I wore my old one till it was not worth a penny, and that wig which I had when I first came is almost done. And I have bespoke a new pair of boots, which I cannot possibly do without, for if you knew what I undergo by going into the country towns to repeat sermons and pray. It happened I and another of my fellow pupils were gone out to repeat a sermon and being without boots we were two hours in a storm of rain and wind. We were lost in a country where we did not know nothing at

---

[1] Minister at Toxteth Park, Liverpool.
[2] Vol. VI. pp. 101, 102.

all of, so that I think it is not only useful but necessary to have a pair. I have, according to your desire, bought a quantity of coals, of which I have bought 10 Hund., which cost 12s. which I borrow'd of my mistress. I should be very glad to know in particular whether Mr Harding preached from that text and whether he has converted any of the new notioners by preaching. I should be very glad if you would desire Mr Harding to let me have a few of his most orthodox sermons to go to repeat. I wish you would be so good as to ask him that favour, if you think it would not be improper. If he could I hope you would send them immediately. Let me know in your next how the affair is, since sermons of the same kind are so very scarce that we can scarce light on a book to write a good sermon out of, but one or another has heard. Pray let me know in this particular the next letter. And I should be very glad if you would send me my watch and send me a box with a few of your best books, which will be the most convenient for me, as soon as possible. And let me know how my brother Robert goes on, whether he is gone to St Helen's School—and if he is pray don't, and I earnestly beg you would board him at William Claughton's, for if you do, so young as he is, he will certainly be ruined ; for I have seen the many dangers and difficulties, and have wondered since how I broke through them ; so that for your own happiness and his everlasting happiness, do not send him thither, for if I thought you would send him thither I should never be easy, etc. So I must beg leave to conclude with my respects, as due.

From your very dutiful son

S. MERCER.

P.S. Dr Father,—I should esteem it not only as a great favour, but as a great honour paid to me, if you would be so good as it is for my interest, to make a present to the doctor of a couple of Cheshire cheeses[1], not strong, but mild and fat which will be very acceptable to the doctor, as he provided me a tutor last year, and I do not know whether he will be paid

[1] Samuel's father was Joseph Mercer, a farmer and cheese factor, of Allerton near Liverpool.

for it, and likewise if you please that I should make a present of something about a crown value to the doctor's Assistant, who, when he should have been taking recreation has been instructing me so that it would be a means of my further improvement, and likewise to send my Dame for she is a widow and she behaves very well to me. I hope, father, you will not forget. And I must beg the favour in particular to send a Cheshire cheese to one of my particular acquaintance, a shop keeper, where I buy my stockings, and where I am positive of it, I am used as if I were almost some of their family, whose son I have under my care to teach Latin, and, who, if it lay in their power, would help me in the greatest extremity, who has made me several handsome presents and sell me their goods, as I have seen with my own eyes—a pair of stockings I have bought 6*d*. cheaper than they have sold to any of our gentlemen—who are very religious people, not those who cant people out of their money, and give them fair words.

This letter is illustrative, not only of the pecuniary difficulties of many of the students in the academies, but also of the willingness of the Tutors to give free tuition to poor youths. An extract from Doddridge's diary evidently refers to the circumstances mentioned by Mercer ; ' Whereas the income of my people and estate, presents included, has not been above a hundred and fifty pounds more than by pupils, of which more than one-tenth has been given in the education of four of my pupils—Walker, B. Strange, Mercer and White.'

Among the students were also John Aikin, Tutor at Warrington, Samuel Merrivale, Tutor at Exeter, and Caleb Ashworth, Doddridge's successor at Daventry.

After twenty-two years' toil, Doddridge, never a strong man, had to leave Northampton, 1751. He died in the following year.

A few years after beginning his work at Northampton,

Doddridge had been approached as to his willingness to be the first Theological Tutor of an academy established under the will of a wealthy Nonconformist, Mr Coward, who died 1738. Mr Coward's trustees supported several young men in Doddridge's academy, but did not seek to direct its management. After Doddridge's death, however, the academy was taken under their control ; Dr Caleb Ashworth of Daventry was appointed the Theological Tutor ; and the academy was moved to Daventry, where it remained till 1789. There were several other removals, and in 1833, in order that the students might attend the Arts course at University College and receive only theological training from their Principal, it was established in Byng Place and was known as Coward's College. This arrangement continued until the union of the three London Colleges in 1850[1].

Development in the second period is really sufficiently shown by this account of Northampton, but Tewkesbury, one of the smaller academies of the period, deserves special mention as having educated two notable dignitaries of the Established Church, Archbishop Secker and Joseph Butler. Samuel Chandler, too, was at Tewkesbury for a time. The Tutor at Tewkesbury, Samuel Jones, was a man of remarkable ability and one to whom both Jennings and Doddridge were indebted in the preparation of their lectures.

One of the entries in the MS. collection of the lives of Dissenting ministers (in Dr Williams's Library) reads as follows :

[1] *Senatus Academicus*, p. 53. List of Academies, no. 26, period II, Appendix No. I.

' About the year 1708 or 9 he (Samuel Jones) began an Academy at Gloucester and then removed to Tewkesbury...and, for the space of twelve years, had a most flourishing Academy, famed for as much learning as any one seminary among the Nonconformists. The Languages and Mathematics were very much studied here. About 100 students were brought up in twelve years.'

The founder of this academy, Samuel Jones, though not an Oxford or Cambridge man, had received a very good education. After having attended two Dissenting Academies in Wales, at Abergavenny (perhaps, however, this was a grammar school) under Roger Griffith, and at Knells (Radnorshire) under John Weaver, an ejected minister and University man, Jones went to Leyden University, 1706. There he came under the influence of some of the most illustrious scholars of the day—among them, Hermann Witsius and James Perizonius. Jones was, therefore, well qualified by university learning to start an academy.

Jones remained at Gloucester until 1712, and then the necessity of obtaining larger premises caused him to go to Tewkesbury. While the academy was still at Gloucester, Thomas Secker (afterwards Archbishop of Canterbury) entered in 1710.

Secker had been under Timothy Jollie at Attercliffe, and, no doubt, moved to Jones' Academy in the hope of obtaining special advantages under him in some branch of his work—just as he, later, moved first to London to study Science under John Eames, F.R.S. (Moorfields—see No. 22, Period II) and then to Paris and Leyden, where he graduated as M.D., and finally, having conformed, to Exeter College, Oxford. It may be conjectured that the subjects in which Secker wished to specialise at Tewkesbury were those allied to biblical study, of which Jones made a special feature, for under Witsius he had spent much time on Jewish Antiquities, Hebrew and Greek Testament and kindred studies. Writing to Dr Watts, Secker says ' I began to learn Hebrew...we read every day two verses apiece in the Hebrew Bible, which we turn into Greek (no one knowing which his verses shall be, though at first it was otherwise).' A wise change of method of reading in class seems to be suggested here.

In the same letter to Watts[1] Secker gives an account of the work done at Tewkesbury. He mentions the usual subjects, amongst which Theology seems to have the chief place. Heereboord's Logic and Locke's *Understanding* are specially named. The parts of his letter dealing with Jones's methods are more interesting and deserve to be quoted at length. ' What Mr Jones dictated to us was but short, containing a clear and brief account of the matter ; references to the places where it was more fully treated of and remarks on, or explications of, the authors cited, when need required it. At our next lecture we gave an account both of what the author quoted and our Tutor said, who commonly gave a larger explication of it and so proceeded to the next thing in order. In the morning the students took Hebrew, Greek and Logic, critical lectures on the Antiquity of the Hebrew Language—corruption of the Scriptures, etc....this is what we first set about in the afternoon, which, being finished, we read a chapter in

[1] See Gibbons' *Memoirs of Dr Isaac Watts*, p. 346 *et seq.*

Greek Testament—after that Mathematics—Algebra and proportion ; first six books of Euclid. This is our daily employment, which in the morning takes about two hours and something more in afternoon. Only on Wednesdays in the morning we read Dionysius's Periegesis, on which we have notes, mostly geographical, but with some criticisms intermixed. In the afternoon (Wednesday) we had no lecture[1].' During college hours Latin had always to be spoken. Secker speaks of the Library ' which is composed for the most part of foreign books, which seem to be very well chosen and are, every day, of great advantage to us.'

Owing, no doubt, to Samuel Jones's education at Leyden, the Theological course at Tewkesbury was more emphasised than the other work, and probably received more attention than was paid to it in other academies. The result of this work was the production of such great scholars and theologians as Joseph Butler and Samuel Chandler.

Butler entered the academy in the Gloucester days and removed to Tewkesbury. While there he read many philosophical and theological works. In 1714 he conformed, and, desiring to take orders in the Established Church, went to Oriel, Oxford, where, he says ' the frivolous lectures quite tired me out[2].' Were they such a contrast to the serious work of the academy ? Chandler, too, was at the academy and formed there

---

[1] Secker's Time-table in 1712 works out as follows :

Morning (2 hours)	*Afternoon* (2–3 hours)	*Evening*
Hebrew	Hebrew Language and Literature	Private
Greek	Greek New Testament	Reading
Logic	Mathematics	

[2] Quoted in Davies' *Account of Tewkesbury Academy,* p. 23.

life-long friendships with Butler and Secker. He, too, did great service in the defence of Christianity and wrote many theological works. He became the most influential and respected minister of the Presbyterian Church, and was honoured with the degree of D.D. by Edinburgh and Aberdeen. Another student to be mentioned is John Bowles, who had, like Secker, been under Jollie. After leaving Tewkesbury, he continued his Law Studies and in 1757 became Lord Chancellor of Ireland.

Other students who filled important positions as ministers or Tutors were Andrew Gifford, Jeremiah Jones, Edward Godwin and Vavasor Griffiths.

Samuel Jones, the Tutor, died October 11th, 1719. He had not had a peaceful time at Tewkesbury, for there, as in other parts of the country, when Sacheverell's preaching and the agitation about the Schism Bill raised the cry of ' The Church in danger,' there were disturbances which threatened to be serious. In spite of these troubles, however, Jones toiled on. The following is Archbishop Secker's estimate of his Tutor. ' Mr Jones, I take to be a man of real piety, great learning and an agreeable temper ; one who is very diligent in instructing all under his care, and very well qualified to give instructions, and whose well-managed familiarity will always make him respected. He is very strict in keeping good orders, and will effectually preserve his pupils from negligence and immorality[1].' Jones won a reputation as a thoroughly good scholar and Tutor. His lectures were not published, but in MS. those on Jewish Antiquities were used by Jennings

[1] *Memoirs of Dr Isaac Watts*, Gibbons, p. 347.

at Kibworth and by Doddridge, who made use of his Ethics lectures also.

After Jones's death the academy was discontinued. There is a tradition which says that the academy was removed to Carmarthen, but probably the only foundation for this is, that the Library was sent there.

One cannot read the accounts of the second period academies without realising that within less than a hundred years from the Conformity legislation the small struggling academies had developed into an important educational system doing a much needed work in the country. There is a great difference between the small early academies, often started diffidently and in some cases in an almost apologetic spirit, and these later academies with their more complete organisation and their specialised studies which made them so successful in competing with the universities.

Doddridge was great not only in his own academy at Northampton but in his influence in the country generally. In his day, to mention Northampton academy was not merely to speak of the best educational centre in the country, it was also to speak of a new education.

The period 1690–1750 was a period of transition. The first period academies, 1662–1690 can only be described as ' classical,' those of the second period 1690–1750 were classical-modern. During the period there gradually strengthened the recognition of the fact—dimly seen by the ejected teachers—that the old aim of education in the grammar schools and the universities, to fit a man to become a clergyman—a clerk— was too narrow. Consequently the academies opened their doors to youths who, not wishing to become professional men, needed a good general education with possibly a knowledge of French or Science as a preparation for a commercial life. By degrees the academy students were divided and there came into being distinct groups taking ' modern ' subjects. More time was therefore given to History, Geography, to various sciences and to modern languages, and these subjects received a definite place in the time-table, and instead of being just read by the students in their rooms each had a lecture period allotted to it. And if often the ' lecture ' consisted in nothing but questioning the students on their reading, or if French were ' read without regard to the pronunciation of which Mr Jennings had no knowledge,' still an advance had been made. Attention has been drawn to the cheapness of the academies, and as time went on their splendid education appealed more and more to the middle classes who were becoming convinced of the power given to them by knowledge. In method, too, changes were made. There seems to have been more care for the individual in the second period academies. The attempt to help backward students in the evening at Northampton is indicative of this, and then, too, the lectures were not merely read with no desire on the part of the lecturer that they should be understood. They were all, as has been noticed, in English and after the lecture, questions and discussions, which seem, during the period, to have developed into debating societies[1] were invited.

[1] Doddridge's Kibworth course, see Appendix No. II; influence of rationalism, see below, p. 145.

Priestley, who went to the Northampton Academy just after the removal to Daventry, occasioned by the death of Doddridge, writes ' In my time the Academy was in a state peculiarly favourable to the serious pursuit of truth, as the students were about equally divided upon every question of much importance, such as liberty and necessity, the sleep of the soul, and all the articles of theological orthodoxy and heresy ; in consequence of which, all these topics were the subject of continual discussion. Our tutors also were of different opinions ; Dr Ashworth taking the orthodox side of every question and Mr Clark, the sub-tutor, that of heresy, though always with the greatest modesty. Our lectures had often the air of friendly conversations on the subjects to which they related. We were permitted to ask whatever questions and to make whatever remarks we pleased, and we did it with the greatest but without any offensive, freedom. The general plan of our studies which may be seen in Dr Doddridge's published lectures was exceedingly favourable to free inquiry, as we were referred to authors on both sides of every question, and even required to give an account of them[1].'

Indeed, the Tutors seem to have been desirous not of cramming their students with facts but of educating them and of training them to think, and what is more, to express their thoughts in their own tongue.

These advances prepared the way for the work of the next period. The wish to give clearer expression to these new educational ideas crystallised into still more definite action about the middle of the 18th century,

[1] Rutt, *Life and Correspondence of Joseph Priestley*, Vol. I. p. 23.

when a very real attempt was made to bring education into closer touch with life. ' Why,' it was asked, ' should youths be trained to be ministers, lawyers and doctors and not be trained to be merchants, clerks and tradesmen ? ' This broader conception of the aim of education received expression in Priestley's *Essay on Education* in the preface of which he says : ' I mean to point out one capital defect in the usual method of educating young gentlemen, who are not designed for any of the learned professions, in places of public and liberal education and at the same time in some measure to supply that defect by giving a delineation of a set of lectures equally useful for any department of life, such as has a nearer connection with their conduct in it and therefore may bid fair to engage their attention and be of more real use to them than any branch of learning to which they have hitherto been made to apply, after they have left the Grammar School[1].'

In accordance with these ideas the modern subjects, and new methods already attempted in the academies of the second period, received more attention. In addition to all the lectures being delivered in English there were lessons in English itself—from being only a vehicle for the communication of knowledge it came to be recognised as a subject worthy of study for its own sake.

This study of English and also of History, Geography and Chemistry was strongly advocated by Priestley[2] who was fortunate in having an opportunity of putting into practice his advanced views on Education in an academy at Warrington, which, because of the

[1] *Essay on Education*, Priestley.
[2] For Priestley's syllabuses, etc., see Appendix VI.

circumstances attending its foundation and the exceedingly broad aims of the directors, was peculiarly fitted to be the institution in which educational experiments, of the nature suggested, might be made.

About 1753–5 the Rev. John Seddon, a young minister in Warrington, began to appeal for subscriptions to start an academy which should be for the education ' of ministers free to follow the dictates of their own judgments in the inquiries after truth, without any undue bias imposed on their understandings ' and which should ' give some knowledge to those who were engaged in commercial life as well as in the learned professions and in the more useful branches of literature[1].' Seddon appealed to churches and to the principal merchants of the northern commercial centres ; in 1754 he had received promises of help from churches as far away as Bristol and Exeter, and from Manchester £94. 10s. 0d., from Liverpool £46. 4s. 0d., Birmingham £44. 12s. 6d., and Warrington £31. 15s. 6d. These sums were contributed by laymen—business men. Their interest in the undertaking is evidence of the need for an education on what might be called a 'commercial' basis.

The undertaking was evidently regarded as most important ; plan succeeded plan, and the discussion seemed endless, but at last, on January 30th, 1757, at a meeting of the supporters of the academy, ' proposals for carrying into execution a plan for the liberal education of youth ' were definitely considered ; trustees appointed ; necessary staff discussed and fees

[1] From *Transactions of Historical Society of Lancashire and Cheshire*, Vol. XI.

arranged. Mr Seddon, as the Secretary, had the arrangements to make. Owing probably to jealousy between Manchester and Liverpool, the academy was to be at Warrington and a suitable house was taken (this house is still standing). It was decided to have four tutors, but only three were appointed—Dr Taylor, of Norwich, ' whose learning was so generally acknowledged that in 1754 all the English and Welsh bishops and archbishops, except four, were among the subscribers to his great Hebrew concordance,' became Tutor in Divinity ; Mr Holt, of Kirkdale, ' whose whole soul was absorbed by his science,' in Natural Philosophy (Mathematics) ; and Mr Dyer, of London, in Languages and polite literature and ' for the present in Moral Philosophy.' Each was to receive from the fund £100 per annum, and from each of the richer students £2 per annum (poorer students were free). In order to make their income suffice for their needs, the tutors (they were non-resident) took boarders into their houses at £15 per annum for those who had two months' vacation and £18 for those who remained the whole year—tea, washing, fire and candles were extra.

Mr Dyer, though appointed, did not go to Warring · ton and Dr Aikin (Mrs Barbauld's father) took his place.

Among the preparations for the academy must be mentioned the endeavours of the Trustees to form a Library ' in some degree correspondent to the extensive plan contemplated.' They were fortunate in obtaining books from a few benefactors, among whom the chief were Dr Percival, of Liverpool, Kendall, of Ulverstone, and the son of Dr Benjamin Grosvenor, of London, who gave all his father's valuable library. A catalogue was printed and is useful as indicating the books of reference used by the students[1].

The academy opened with three students on October 20th, 1757. In accordance with the customary practice, the Divinity Tutor took the position of Head of the academy. Unfortunately, Dr Taylor became involved in a quarrel with the Trustees, and this unhappy circumstance, no doubt, proved a drawback to the academy which did not become so large as its founders had hoped. The entries average 14 a year, 393 students being trained there during its short existence, 1757–1783.

A list in Vol. IX of the *Monthly Repository* enables an analysis of the students taking various courses to be made—it is as follows :

Entered for Law		22
,,	,, Medicine	24
,,	,, Divinity	52
,,	,, Commerce	98
Course not specified		197

' Commerce ' seems to indicate the course taken by merchants, bankers, and those designed for the leading positions in large commercial companies. Brewers, shop-keepers—all ' tradesmen '—are among the ' unspecified ' as also are many who later entered the army and some who were styled ' country gentlemen.' These had a good ' general ' education[2].

[1] See Appendix IV for Analysis of Catalogue and full list of books, under heads (1) History, Geography, Voyages, etc., (2) Miscellaneous.
[2] See also Appendix V.

The Tutors[1] at this academy are particularly interesting and seem to justify the following eulogistic remark, ' At Warrington Academy were collected some of the noblest literati of their day. Here the free thought of English Presbyterianism first began to crystallise into the Unitarian theology. Here for a time was the centre of the liberal politics and the literary taste of the entire country[2].' One can imagine the life in Warrington in those days—the theological discussions, the political and social talks of the tutors, the literary enthusiasm of Dr Aikin's daughter and her friends.

In 1761 Dr Taylor died, and Dr Aikin took his place. Dr Aikin's successor was Joseph Priestley. In

[1] Divinity ..   ..   John Taylor, D.D., 1757–1761.
                                            John Aikin, D.D., 1761–1780.
                                            Nicholas Clayton, D.D., 1780–1783.

Classics ..   ..   John Aikin, D.D., 1758–1761.

Languages and Belles Lettres ..   J. Priestley, LL.D., 1761–1767.

Languages and Natural History   J. Reinhold Forster, LL.D. 1767–1770 (?).
                                            La Tour, 1770–(?).

Belles Lettres ..   ..   ..   John Seddon, 1767–1770.
                                            Wm. Enfield, LL.D., 1770–1783

Classics ..   ..   Gilbert Wakefield, A.B., 1779–1783.
                                            Pendlebury Houghton, 1778–1779 (Assistant).

Mathematics ..   ..   ..   John Holt, 1757–1772.
                                            George Walker, F.R.S., 1772–1774.
                                            Wm. Enfield, LL.D., 1774–1783.

Rector Academiae   ..   ..   John Seddon, 1767–1770.
                                            Wm. Enfield, 1770–1783.

[2] *Transactions of Historical Society of Lancashire and Cheshire,* Vol. XI.

the following year the academy moved to larger and more convenient buildings in Academy Place, and there it entered upon its period of greatest prosperity. Priestley was succeeded by John Reinhold Forster, a German scholar and naturalist. Forster went with Captain Cook in his second voyage round the world and was considered one of the best botanists of his day. He lectured in Natural History and Modern Languages and took the junior forms in Latin and Greek. While at Warrington he published a few books, among which were translations of Bougainville's *Voyage Round the World* and of Baron Riedesel's *Travels through Sicily*. According to a report issued by the Trustees, 1770, ' foreigners, from time to time, were engaged to fill Reinhold Forster's place ' ; but there is only one name given, Mr La Tour, who is believed to have taught drawing and book-keeping, in addition to Modern Languages. The Rev. George Walker, who succeeded Holt, stayed only two years ; he afterwards became Tutor of Divinity at Manchester New College ; Gilbert Wakefield, the Editor of Lucretius, ' claims rank among the foremost of Cambridge men who have thrown light on the ancient Classics.' Before his death in 1770, Seddon had become Rector and had lectured on Oratory and grammar. His lectures were continued by Dr Enfield, who was untiring in his work while the academy lasted. Certainly, the Trustees did their best to secure good men. Of all the Tutors, Dr Aikin and Dr Priestley, were the most important, and an idea of this academy, which was so far in advance of its predecessors, will best be gained by an account of their methods

Dr Aikin's ' passion for Literature ' led his father to take him from a foreign merchant's office (where he had acquired ' extraordinary facility in French ') and to allow him to continue his education at a school kept by a retired actor with a taste for declamation, which he seems to have imparted to Aikin.   Later, in 1732, Aikin became a pupil under Doddridge and then proceeded to Aberdeen, where he obtained the degree of D.D. and whence he returned to be assistant at Northampton.   He had, therefore, had some academical experience before going to Warrington.   Gilbert Wakefield, for a short time his colleague, says he was ' a gentleman whose endowments as a man and as a scholar it is not easy to exaggerate.   His acquaintance with all true evidence of revelation, with morals, politics, metaphysics was most accurate and extensive —he knew Hebrew, French, Greek and Latin.'   Aikin first lectured in classics 1758–61 and then as Lecturer in Divinity, became head of the academy 1761–1780— he was, therefore, connected with it for almost the whole period of its existence.   Writing to the *Monthly Repository* in 1812, an old student gives many interesting details about Dr Aikin's work[1].   The method he adopted in his classical lectures is described at some length.   It was his plan to give first a general account of the author, the time in which he lived, scope of his subject and his treatment of it.   The students, each in turn, read the book through with the guidance of the tutor, who ' cleared up difficulties and illustrated the scope and tendency of the argument with uncommon clearness and precision.'   It is recorded that Dr Aikin

[1] *Monthly Repository*, Vol. VIII. p. 166.

usually selected, not those books most commonly taken in schools, but those which the students might not otherwise read and those which were connected with their other studies—the parts of Herodotus which might illustrate what they read in the Old Testament about Assyria and Egypt and Justinian's Institutes when there were several reading for the Bar. Passages from modern poetry, in which Dr Aikin was widely read and which he delighted to quote, often served as illustrations of the subject in hand. The Doctor was always anxious to be understood ; at the end of a lecture, he invariably added ' Gentlemen, have I explained the subject to your satisfaction ? ' and then waited to meet any difficulty which might be stated.

The Divinity students were required to write exercises and take them to the Saturday morning lecture. ' First year, essays on subjects connected with their course, or Latin Translation or Free Composition—second and third year, schemes of sermons, fourth year sermons and critical dissertations. These were read by the student and criticised by the Tutor. After the exercises were examined he would turn to some of the finest passages of the English poets— Milton, Pope, Thomson, Young, and Akenside, and, having first read a considerable portion, he heard each of the students read in order and pointed out their defects. This lecture was often the most satisfactory and improving of any in the whole week[1].'

The same writer gratefully remembers the ' frequent small parties to drink tea with him ' that Dr Aikin had.

[1] *Monthly Repository*, Vol. VIII. pp. 166–7.

On these occasions the students were encouraged to discuss the various topics which interested them.

These details leave us in no doubt as to the value of Dr Aikin's work. His lectures must have been really interesting—Latin and Greek must have been vastly different from the Latin and Greek of the old days and of many of the schools of his day.

More important, however, was his work in English. By the ' free, familiar conversation ' at his tea-parties ; by discussion after the lectures ; and by that delightful Saturday morning class, Dr Aikin was doing a great work in remedying that serious defect in the early academies so much regretted by Defoe. As Principal, he may be regarded as responsible for the newer subjects which were introduced ; but it is chiefly to Joseph Priestley that the honour of modernising the curriculum belongs. Priestley was a member of the staff only from 1761–67, but in that short time he revolutionised the work. Appointed as Lecturer in Languages and Belles Lettres he undertook subjects such as Chemistry, Anatomy, etc., History and Geography, so that when he left, two men divided his work ; Forster taking Languages and Natural History, and Seddon, Belles Lettres.

Priestley (born 1733) was adopted by his aunt in 1742 and sent to a large free school, where he learnt Latin and Greek, and Hebrew on holidays ; ' with a view to trade,' he writes, ' I learned French, Italian and High Dutch.' He was sent to Daventry 1752 under Dr Caleb Ashworth (Doddridge's successor). His account of his education is too interesting to be omitted ; ' between my leaving the grammar school and going to the academy, I went two days a week to Mr Hagger-stone, a Dissenting minister. Of him I learnt geometry, algebra, various branches of mathematics, theoretical and practical, and read Gravesande's *Elements of Natural Philosophy*, Watts's *Logic* and Locke's *Human Understanding*, and made such proficiency in these branches that when I was admitted at the Academy I was excused all the studies of the first year and a great part of those of the second. While at the grammar school I learned Mr Annet's *Shorthand*.... Among other things at this time I had a great aversion to plays and romances, so that I never read any works of this kind, except *Robinson Crusoe*, until I went to the Academy[1].'

Priestley remained at the Daventry Academy for three years, 1752–1755. In 1758 he took charge of a church at Nantwich. Here also, he not only had a school but gave what seem to have been courses of popular lecturers on scientific subjects to adults. One course was on the Use of the Globes. The proceeds (10s. 6d. for twelve lectures) and the school fees enabled him to ' purchase a few books, some philosophical instruments, a small air-pump, electrical machine, etc., and by entertaining the parents and friends with experiments in which the scholars were generally the operators and sometimes the lecturers too, I extended the reputation of the school[2].' It was for the use of these scholars that Priestley wrote his *Rudiments of English Grammar, adapted to the use of schools, with observations on style*, which he afterwards had printed,

---

[1] *Life and Correspondence of Joseph Priestley*, J. T. Rutt, p. 13 *et seq.*
[2] *Ibid.* Vol. I.

and a copy of which is to be found in the present library at Warrington. In the preface he writes: ' The propriety of introducing English grammar into English schools cannot be disputed, a competent knowledge of our own language being both useful and ornamental in every profession, and a critical knowledge of it absolutely necessary to all persons of liberal education ....though the grammar school be, on all accounts, the most proper place for learning it, how many grammar schools have we, and of no small reputation, which are destitute of all provision for the regular teaching of it[1] ? ' At the end of the book are ' examples of English composition,' and among these are to be found extracts from the Bible, Addison, Young, Bolingbroke, Hume, Swift, Pope and others. Wolsey's farewell is the only one from Shakespeare.

So much for Priestley's work at Nantwich—work which prepared him for that at the academy to which he went in 1761. He was appointed Tutor of Languages and Belles Lettres, and, judging from a letter written after he went to Warrington, he must have been well occupied. He writes (probably about 1765): ' I think myself honoured by Mr Blackburn's inquiry after my department in the Academy. Besides the three courses of Lectures of which an account is given in the Essay[2] I teach Latin, Greek, French and Italian and read Lectures on the Theory of Languages and Universal grammar, on Oratory and Philosophical criticism and also on Civil Law[3].'

[1] Priestley, *Rudiments of English Grammar*, Preface, p. viii.

[2] *I.e.* Priestley's *Essay on a Liberal Education*.

[3] *Life and Correspondence of Joseph Priestley*, J. T. Rutt, Vol. i, p. 46.

Priestley worked at Warrington from 1761–67—teaching almost every subject in the curriculum and doing his utmost to make the education of real value to the students. During this time he attended a course of lectures on chemistry delivered at the academy by a learned apothecary and chemist, Dr Turner of Liverpool. He also wrote and published courses of lectures, essays on educational and social questions and theological works. The establishment of a printing press by Eyres in Warrington synchronised with the foundation of the academy, and no doubt each influenced the other—the academy found work for Eyres, and the fact of there being so good a printer in the neighbourhood encouraged the tutors to print their essays and translations.

Priestley's *Essay on a Course of Liberal Education for Civil and Active Life* (1765) is noteworthy for its insistence upon the necessity of altering the curriculum so as to suit the changing needs of the day. He says—' Formerly, none but the clergy were thought to have any occasion for learning. It was natural therefore that the whole plan of education, from the grammar school to the finishing at the university should be calculated for their use[1].' He goes on to show that times have changed, that life is more complex and that consequently the supine inattention with which affairs were formerly conducted is no longer safe and that a ' different and better furniture of mind is requisite to be brought into the business of life.' This Priestley sees is ' certainly a call upon us to examine the state of education in this country.' He then proceeds to

---

[1] *Essay on Liberal Education*, p. 2.

advocate a wide study of history[1] (with which geography is to be closely connected) and requires that a youth going through the courses he outlines should know sufficient Latin as to enable him to read the easier classics and to understand and use ' the more difficult English words which are derived from the Latin[2].' A good knowledge of French he considers very necessary ; the more useful branches of practical mathematics should be known, and if possible he should have some knowledge of algebra and geometry, which are ' indispensable in every plan of liberal education[2].' Priestley was no mere idle theorist. His work at the academy proves conclusively his serious interest in education, and accounts of the reforms he was attempting evidently reached other tutors, for there are requests from some of them for his advice on certain matters relating to teaching. Priestley's replies show, not only what methods he employed, but also the considerations which guided him in their adoption. Writing to a Mr Caleb Rotherham under date February 14th, 1766, he says: ' I introduced lectures on history and general policy, laws and constitutions of England and on the history of England. This I did in consequence of observing that though most of our pupils were young men designed for situations in civil and active life, every article in the plan of their education was adapted to the learned professions. In order to recommend such studies as I introduced, I composed an " Essay on a Course of Liberal Education for Civil and Active Life[3]." '

[1] See Appendix VI for extracts from course of lectures.

[2] *Essay on Liberal Education*, pp. 18, 19.

[3] *Life and Correspondence of Joseph Priestley*, ed. J. T. Rutt, Vol. I. p. 50.

To the same friend he says : ' I made use of Holmes'
Latin Grammar....My English grammar was not
ready in time enough for me to make a trial of it.
It has been out of print two or three years and I shall
not consent to its being reprinted [he changed his mind],
Lowth's is much better ; but I question whether it will
signify much to teach any English grammar. Making
the scholars compose dialogues, themes etc., correcting
their bad English and making occasional remarks, I
always found of most real use. Let them write fair
copies of the English of many of their lessons and omit
no opportunity of making them write in their own
language. This you will find pleasant to yourself, and
of prodigious service to your pupils. Do not fail to
teach geography along with the classics, for by this
means your pupils will, indirectly, acquire much real
knowledge. I had a little school library, consisting
chiefly of books of natural and civil history, with
books of travel which I made them read (as a favour)
with the map before them[1].'

Such were Priestley's ideas ; such was his work ; its
results cannot be so definitely set down. It can only
be said that his influence was very great. There was
first, of course, the result of his work in the academy
in the training of the young men under him. Then,
through the continuance of his work by those who
succeeded him there was carried on his attempt to
modernise, to ' humanise ' the curriculum. Again,
through his letters and essays and through the reputation gained by the academy, the influence was spread,

[1] *Life and Correspondence of Joseph Priestley*, ed. J. T. Rutt,
Vol. I. p. 64.

it is not too much to say, throughout England. And, finally, the growth of a new idea about education (an idea which still persists) may perhaps be traced to this work of Priestley—the idea of the necessity of a Dissenting education for lay Dissenters. Priestley certainly made the curriculum suitable for laymen outside the learned professions, and by so doing, he enlarged the borders of the Dissenting academies, and probably hastened the expression of what may have been felt before—-the *need* of a Dissenting education for Dissenters ; that is to say, that what in 1662 was a makeshift, an adaptation to changing circumstances, became, about 1800, a necessity. Expression is given to this idea in a letter on the ' Necessity of a Dissenting education for Lay Dissenters ' from ' A friend to the permanence of Unitarian Dissent ' in the *Monthly Repository* for 1812[1]. This may not, of course, have been the first time the idea was expressed ; but it was one of the earliest expressions of it.

As before mentioned, the year after Priestley went to Warrington the academy had to seek larger premises. A new academy and houses for the tutors were built, and this undertaking involved the Trustees in a debt of almost £2000. This difficulty was increased by the gradual dropping off of the promised subscriptions. This, suggests the writer in the *Monthly Repository* quoted above, was due partly to the quarrel between Dr Taylor and the Trustees and partly to the somewhat natural apathy of the subscribers, to whom no account of the annual expenditure was sent and who were probably ignorant, not only of the manner in which

---

[1] *Monthly Repository*, Vol. x. p. 286.

their money was spent, but also of the work the academy was doing. The lack of funds prevented adequate salaries being paid to the tutors, and several of them, because of actual necessity, had to seek other work. This was the reason of Priestley's removal to Leeds in 1767, and it was also the reason for Mr Seddon's undertaking to give various lectures, and for the offers from other tutors to take extra work. New regulations and one or two changes made in the administration in 1767 throw light upon the discipline of the academy. The account[1] is as follows : ' To remove all danger of dissatisfaction with any of the tutors, a person unconnected with the conduct of any branch of education was engaged to provide the commons for the students, and a regular code of laws was drawn up (a printed copy given to each student, who was explicitly to promise obedience). The Trustees appointed, in the person of Mr Seddon, a Rector Academiae, whose particular office it should be to superintend the discipline and morals of the students.... An exact weekly register was to be read over by the Rector every Saturday afternoon publicly before all students and such reprimands and admonitions to be given by him and the tutors as to them should seem necessary.... the Tutor is to proceed to appoint the delinquents a proper exercise and on no account to dispense with the performance of it.' A report, in the case of the delinquents, was to be sent once a quarter to the parents or guardians, and if these measures did not suffice expulsion was to follow. After Mr Seddon's death Mr Enfield, who had been appointed Tutor in Belles Lettres in 1770 and had

[1] *Monthly Repository*, Vol. VIII. p. 427.

volunteered to take Mathematics after George Walker left in 1774, became Rector. He was quite in accord with the new methods, and as his *Speaker* and *Exercises in Elocution* testify, was as anxious as Aikin and Priestley to train the students in the use of their mother tongue. He continued the special Saturday morning class, and ' in order to encourage among the students at large an alacrity to engage in voluntary exercises, he, in conjunction with his friend Dr Aikin, Junior (who settled at Warrington as a surgeon, and continued the course of lectures in anatomy, physiology, chemistry etc.), promoted the formation of societies or clubs for improvement in elocution and composition. They both became members and took turns in sub-mitting to general discussion, essays of their own.'

During all this time the academy was in debt and the number of students gradually decreased, until in 1783, it having been decided to open a new academy in Manchester, the Warrington Academy, which had done such magnificent work for about five-and-twenty years, was closed. The academy in Manchester, called ' Manchester New College,' was closely connected with the Warrington Academy. The Warrington library was transferred to Manchester ; the first Principal, Dr Barnes, was trained at Warrington ; and the second, Rev. G. Walker had been tutor there.

Though at different times situated in various places (Manchester, York, Manchester, London, Oxford) Manchester New College has had an uninterrupted existence and is now represented by its lineal descendant, Manchester College, Oxford. Until 1853 it remained an institution for training both ministers and laymen

—since then, its work has been theological only. Manchester College has now the old Warrington library and the minutes of the Trustees. The Warrington window in the present library commemorates the connection between the two institutions. Manchester College claims descent not only from Chorlton's Academy (as stated in the *Victoria County History of Lancashire*) but also from Frankland's Academy at Rathmell[1]. For this claim there is no justification whatever. Even if it be allowable to group together, as in the appendix referred to, Rathmell, Chorlton's, Whitehaven, Bolton and Kendal as the Northern Academy (there was really no connection between Chorlton's and Whitehaven or between Bolton and Kendal), it is not possible to regard Warrington, which was an entirely new foundation, as descended from these earlier academies.

It seems natural that the first big attempt to give a 'business education' should have been made in the district most influenced by the 18th century development of industry. A similar attempt was made in the south-west of England and seems to have been on the whole successful. The West of England Academy situated at Taunton 1672–1759 (Period I, No. 17) was closed on the removal of the last Tutor, Dr Amory, to London. After he had gone the Nonconformists of the district decided to establish ' a seminary not for the ministry alone but also for other learned professions and for civil life.' A house in Exeter was given and the library from Taunton removed to the new academy, which was placed under the direction of

[1] See appendix on Ancestry of Manchester College in *Proceedings and Addresses on the Opening of Manchester College, Oxford.*

Samuel Merivale, who had been under Doddridge at Northampton.

The MS. account of academies in Dr Williams' Library gives the total number of students at Exeter as ninety-three. Among those whose calling is given are

6 attorneys or barristers.

4 ministers[1].

7 physicians.

24 merchants or ' trade.'

7 navy or navy office men.

13 esquires.

2 apothecaries.

3 army men.

This academy therefore aimed at supplying the broad, modern education given at Warrington, as also did the ' less literary seminary ' started about the same time in London.

This, no doubt, does not complete the list of institutions working on the same lines. Among the Quakers and other Nonconformist bodies there were in all probability similar plans put into execution during the same period. It is to be regretted that just when this further and very important development was contemplated the academies forgot the breadth of view with which they had started and began to require from their students acceptance of definite creeds. It was probably owing to this departure from their original practice

[1] A list in the *Monthly Repository*, Vol. XII., is different; 12 ministers are mentioned and only 49 names are given.

that the academies gradually declined. As the 18th century closed they seem to have become institutions more bent upon giving a training in the principles of particular Nonconformist bodies rather than upon giving the best liberal education obtainable at the time, with the result that they no longer offered so striking a contrast to the other educational systems of their day.

III

THE PLACE OF THE DISSENTING ACADEMIES AMONG THE EDUCATIONAL SYSTEMS IN ENGLAND

Beginning at the time when the Uniformity Legislation was undermining the existing school system built up by Elizabeth and the early Stuarts on such remnants of the old system as survived the ravages of Henry VIII and Edward VI, the academies were the result of an effort to give education where it was withheld. At first, merely an expedient of the moment, they, later, became a definite and necessary part of the educational machinery of their day. Differing from all other centres of learning—unique both in aim and accomplishment—they constitute a separate educational system—an educational system, moreover, which deserves no mean place among the various systems of this country.

Though comparatively small, the academies were thoroughly active. Their tutors were first-rate men ; all of them real students who gave themselves wholeheartedly to the work they had in hand. Such men would make great demands upon their students, and there is abundant evidence that discipline was maintained and that measures were taken to secure honest work.

The academical system of education was short-lived—a ' distributary ' which, a little further down the course, returned to the main river. But the ' distributary ' accomplished much, not only fertilising the land through which it passed, but after its return purifying the main stream and quickening its sluggish flow.

The predominating influence of 18th century thought was Rationalism, and the academies, Puritan and Realistic as they were, were naturally much affected thereby. Discussions which were the natural consequence of a belief in an appeal to reason played an important part in the academies, and indeed so much importance was attached not only to the weekly disputations but to the impromptu discussions after lectures and to those in the students' own rooms that it is not too much to say that with many tutors the aim was rather to cultivate sound judgment than to impart information. In one of his essays[1] Mark Pattison, writing of the period 1688–1830, says : ' In that Age higher education acquired its practical aim, an aim in which the development of the understanding and the acquisition of knowledge are considered secondary objects to the formation of the sound secular judgment of the "scholar and the gentleman" of the old race of schoolmasters.' It is in the academies that this new practical aim is first seen. The writings of Locke were widely read in the academies, and undoubtedly exercised a tremendous influence there. The result of these discussions and of this aim was that academy-trained men took a foremost part in the controversies of the

[1] *Essays*, Vol. II. p. 13.

day. Two of the greatest defenders of Christianity, Chandler and Butler, against the attacks of the Deists, were students in a Dissenting Academy. In his *Studies Subsidiary to Butler*, Mr Gladstone says : ' All the theology of *Butler's Analogy* is derived straight from the Holy Scriptures and ends, as well as begins, with them. Butler never but once quotes a theologian, and that only in one of the notes. With regard to the exclusiveness of his habit of quoting from Holy Scriptures it seems probable that his education as a Presbyterian Dissenter may have done much to form the habit of his mind[1].'

Besides theological writers the academies trained preachers who could afterwards deal with controverted points, and certainly this freedom of discussion was partly responsible for the spread of Unitarianism. The non-theological students also, in various walks of life, gave expression day by day to ideas which had been formed under the influence of the Dissenting education they had received. Among these the influence of Defoe was the greatest, and though it cannot be claimed that either his general literature or his pamphlet-writing was due to his academy education, nevertheless each would no doubt have been different had he been educated, say, at Oxford.

The influence of the academies on English thought and life as a whole was that of a modified Puritanism. In general they stood for independence of thought, but at the same time objected to freedom of action, that is, many of them looked far more askance at departure from received Puritan custom in small details of conduct

---

[1] *Studies Subsidiary to Butler*, p. 108.

than at the acceptance of heterodox opinions. In spite of much deplorable narrowness, their firm stand for broad principles, their sober earnestness and their high moral tone had, to say the least, a salutary effect upon the country.

But in addition to exerting this general Puritan influence they made a very definite impression on education in particular. In this connection probably the most important statement that can be made about them is that they developed, that throughout the whole course of their existence they steadily advanced. The significance of this lies in the fact that the other educational systems show no development whatever—that they were moreover not merely at a standstill but were steadily declining. Abundant and conclusive proof of this is found whenever reliable reference is made to the condition of education in the grammar schools or Universities in the 18th century. Every historian of the Universities or of the public schools when dealing with the period following the Restoration writes of 'the decay which became so evident in the middle of the 18th century,' of the period 'at which the Universities reached the lowest depths of attainment and discipline.'

Writing of St Paul's School, Mr M. F. J. McDonnell says : ' The intellectual blight which in the 18th century fell over Oxford and Cambridge and many of the public schools, did not leave St Paul's unaffected[1],' and Mr A. F. Leach says that though very successful towards the end of the 17th century, owing probably to Charles II's plan of building a palace at Winchester,

[1] *History of St Paul's School*, M. F. J. McDonnell, p. 296.

the school there sank in the 18th century to the ' lowest
depths of depression[1].' The decay began with the
reaction against Puritanism at the Restoration—a
reaction as marked in the schools and Universities as
at the Court. All that savoured of Puritanism was
out of fashion—devotion to learning no less than
abhorrence of pleasure-seeking.

In his description of Oxford after 1660 Antony Wood
shows clearly that it was held to be a point of honour
to make everything as different as possible from what
had obtained during the ' Intervall.' This was seen
not only in such matters as the return to ' May-games,
morrises, revells etc.' so loathed by the ' precise party,'
but in the altering of University regulations ; in the
discontinuing of many lectures and in an exaggerated
mode of life which hated lectures, disputations and
books and delighted in coffee houses, gossiping and
plays. ' Till the Act of Conformity was published,'
writes Wood, ' the Presbyterian preachers laboured
much to keep their disciples together and to strive by
their fluent praying and preaching to make that way
used by the prelaticall party ridiculous. And really,
had not the said Act taken place, which drew over very
many to their (*i.e.* the prelaticall, the Church) party,
they would have found themselves much weakened.'
After the Conformity Legislation, however, the Independents and Presbyterians had to leave the
Universities, and Wood goes on to describe the state
of things in Oxford which ensued. ' They seldom
preached....which made many think they would not
venter to do it for feare they should be disrellisht and

[1] *A History of Winchester College*, A. F. Leach, p. 367.

find not that applause which the Presbyterians and those educated in the Intervall did.' This refers to the services at St Mary's. The actual work of the Universities was discontinued too: 'As the lectures of Divinity were neglected, so those of the Civill Law and what was done at all, was by a deputy. The Medicine likewise was neglected....and as for the Greek lecture the reader thereof....read scarce one lecture from this year till about 1664[1].' As a matter of fact in 1660 the Church returned to her own, and having defined her borders and placed those outside her communion under civil disabilities she settled down in the firm conviction that the House of Stuart once more on the throne, everything would go well. The majority of the country clergy were fox-hunting squires who cared nothing for learning and who therefore made no demands upon the Universities. It was not long before those who required a sound education went either to the Dissenting Academies or to foreign Universities—Oxford and Cambridge were of no use. In his *Studies in Oxford History chiefly in the Eighteenth Century* Green gives an account of life at Oxford which was an 'imitation of High Life in London.' 'Education,' he writes, 'may be found anywhere save in the lecture-room[2].' The writings of 18th century men acquainted with the Universities leave no doubt as to the general opinion about them. Chesterfield, writing to his son, 1749, said that Cambridge 'is sunk into the lowest obscurity and the existence of Oxford would not

---

[1] *Life and Times of Antony Wood*, Clark, Vol. I. pp. 360, 361.

[2] *Studies in Oxford History chiefly in the Eighteenth Century* (Oxf. Hist. Soc.), J. R. Green, p. 30.

be known if it were not for the treasonable spirit
publicly avowed and often excited there.' Gibbon's
censure of Magdalen and indeed of the whole University of Oxford is well known. There is probably
little doubt that his statements were exaggerated and
that the condition of the College and of the University
was not so appalling as it appears in his pages, but
Gibbon was by no means the only man who, looking
back on his career at Oxford, was constrained to admit
that he had done little or no work, and what is more
important, that the University had demanded practically nothing from him. Adam Smith, at Balliol from
1740–46, says he sought in vain for the proper means
of being taught the sciences which it is 'the proper
business of these incorporate bodies to teach.' Southey
was told by one of his tutors that if he had any studies
of his own he had better pursue them, 'for you won't
learn anything from my lectures, sir.' While at Oriel,
Butler, who was acquainted with serious lectures at
Tewkesbury Academy and with the voluntary, strenuous work of the students, wrote : 'we are obliged to
mis-spend so much time in attending frivolous lectures
and unintelligible disputations that I am quite tired
out with such a disagreeable way of trifling.' Many
writers refer to the worse than useless Latin disputations
which continued in the Universities till the beginning
of the 19th century, and at Oriel one a week was required
until 1857 ! Undergraduates were in the habit of
memorising ' strings,' as lists of questions and answers
composing a dispute were called, in readiness for their
' determination ' for the B.A. degree. These strings
were handed down from one generation of students to

another, and many who used them had no idea of the meaning of the Latin which they ' declaimed[1].'

When the Honours Schools were instituted (1800) Sidney Smith wrote: ' If Oxford is become at last sensible of the miserable state to which it was reduced, as everybody else was out of Oxford, and if it is making serious efforts to recover from the degradation into which it was plunged a few years past, the good wishes of every respectable man must go with it.' These efforts at reform were not made until the end of the 18th century. ' If 1700 witnessed the University's greatest inactivity and degradation, 1800 saw it beginning that system of education which led the way to higher and nobler intellectual efforts[2] '

Before 1800 there had been, practically speaking, no attempt at reform. In his *Vindication of Magdalen College from the Aspersions of Mr Gibbon* the Rev. James Hurdie gives the work required of an undergraduate in that college, about the middle of the 18th century, for ' collections ' or term-end examinations. ' In 1st year he must be proficient in, the 1st term, Sallust and characters of Theophrastus; 2nd term, Vergil *Aen.* I–VI, first 3 books of Zenophon's Anabasis; 3rd term, *Aen.* last VI books, Anabasis, the last IV; 4th Term, The Gospels of St Matthew and St Mark[3].' The only change in the next three years is in the set books and in the addition of Greek authors. There was, therefore, no examination in anything but classics, and there is no doubt that Latin and Greek

[1] See account in *Reminiscences of Oxford* (Oxf. Hist. Soc.).

[2] *Studies in Oxford History chiefly in the Eighteenth Century,* Green, p. 240.

[3] *Reminiscences of Oxford* (Oxf. Hist. Soc.), p. 136.

still occupied most of an undergraduate's time. It is
true that some attention was given to logic and ethics
and also to geometry and physics, but the work done
seems to have been very slight. Letters from Henry
Fleming, an undergraduate at Queen's, who entered in
July 1678, show the kind of work he was doing. In
September 1678 he wrote: ' My tutor reads to me once
for the most part every day and sometimes twice in
Sanderson's Logick[1], which booke is all he reads to me
as yet wherein I have read two of ye first bookes and
part of ye third. And in spaire hours from Logick I
read Lucius Florus, Sallus and such histories, out of
which I write collections. And for exercise I make
none yet, but such as all ye scholars make which is
verses every Saturday during ye terme and sometimes
declames[2].' In May 1679 he tells his father that having
read all Sanderson's Logick he has to begin Ethicks and
that in the afternoon he will continue Latin histories.
On Dec. 1st of that year he writes: ' My tutor reads to
me now a compendium of Geometry having done with
Logick and Ethicks[3].' A compendium of 'physicks'
was begun in Aug. 1680.

From a comparison of the Universities and academies
it is clear that while the former continued to give an
essentially classical education, the academies paid more
and more attention to science and to modern languages
and later to 'commercial' subjects. In other words,
the Universities and academies differed fundamentally
in their opinion as to what constituted a ' liberal '

---

[1] This was of course in Latin.
[2] *The Flemings in Oxford* (Oxf. Hist. Soc.), Vol. I. p. 262.
[3] *Ibid*. p. 304.

education. The Universities held that the more education was removed from the ordinary activities of life, the more liberal it was ; that liberal or ' culture ' studies were those which were if not useless, at least definitely non-utilitarian. Moreover, under the influence of Ciceronianism, the ' culture ' studies did not include the broad, literary study advocated by the Renaissance humanists, but merely the narrow, pedantic training in classics and formal logic. However anxious a few enthusiasts might be to introduce reforms, there was always a sufficiently strong majority in the Universities to ensure the continuance of the traditional methods. As we have seen, the earliest attempts at reform were made in the 16th and 17th centuries, but though Savile, Lucas, Camden and others founded professorships the general attitude of the Universities remained unchanged. Indeed the history of the Universities even during the 19th century shows that though definitely utilitarian subjects had been prescribed, it had very often been possible for the professors, to whom the framing of the syllabuses had been left, to make the work done in those subjects so narrow and pedantic as to defeat the end the reformers had in view. In other words, the spirit in the Universities has remained practically unchanged ; much of the work is pedantic still. It is true that now Humanistic Studies such as English Literature and History have a definite place, yet the work is often so detailed and specialised as to be anything but humanistic in spirit. The academies on the other hand held that for an education to be liberal it was imperative that it should be in touch with life and should therefore include as many utilitarian subjects as possible. As has been seen, English early received attention as also did French, and in some cases German, Italian and Spanish ; history and geography came to be quite regularly taught ; while 'science' in some academies was the most important subject. But the difference between the two educational systems is seen not so much in the introduction into the academies of ' modern ' subjects and methods as in the fact that among the Nonconformists there was a totally different spirit at work from that found in the Universities. The spirit animating the Dissenters was that which had moved Ramus and Comenius in France and Germany and which in England had actuated Bacon and later Hartlib and his circle. The academies were the first educational institutions in England to put into practice the realistic theories which had found expression in the works of a series of writers from Rabelais and Montaigne, Mulcaster and Elyot to Bacon and Comenius, Milton and Petty. It was in the academies alone that, while the Universities remained mediaeval in outlook, an attempt was made to meet the changing needs of the time. In the 16th century the Courtly Academies had endeavoured to satisfy the demand on the part of the nobility for an education which the Universities could not give. In the 18th century the Dissenting Academies strove to satisfy the needs of the upper middle class for a practical modern education which the Universities made no effort to supply. There is a further point of similarity between these two types of academies. The Dissenting Academies were not less successful in making their conception of what constituted a good middle-class education seem the only one possible, than the Courtly Academies were in making the scholar-gentleman ideal fashionable. In the 18th century *the* education to be sought was an academy education. Moreover, it was an education which was obtainable nowhere but in these academies. They are important not merely because they gave a new education but for the fact that they showed the people of England that it was no longer necessary to depend solely upon the old institutions for learning.

In so far then as they taught ' modern ' subjects, and employed the newest methods advocated by the educational reformers, and opened their doors to the ' people,' they exerted a true realistic influence, and thus became the forerunners of the modern Universities in our commercial centres. In this respect, as in others, they may be compared with the schools of the Pietists in Germany, which under Francke and his followers prepared the way for the Realschulen, for there can be no doubt that just as the Pietists carried on the work of Comenius in Germany, so the Dissenters put into practice the theories of Comenius' English followers, Hartlib, Milton and Petty.

Reference has already been made to the extent to which Locke was read in the academies[1]. There is no doubt that the influence of Rationalism and the remarkable freedom of inquiry which was allowed in the academies were responsible for the spread of Unitarianism, and this led to the Tutors requiring from the students on entering, subscription to a definite

[1] It is interesting to note that Locke's writings were censured in Oxford, 1703, and reading of the *Essay on Human Understanding* forbidden.

creed. This narrowing of their borders, together with the general decline in Nonconformity towards the end of the 18th century, was the cause of the decay of the academies as centres of general learning. Those founded at the close of the century, like the new college in Hackney in which Priestley was interested, and which was founded about 1788, were definitely denominational, and indeed owing to the influence of this Dissenting Educational system there grew the idea that denominational schools for youths not entering the ministry were as necessary as denominational colleges designed to give ministerial training.

Before the decline of the academies their successful adoption of realistic subjects and methods had drawn considerable attention to the subject of education. By the middle of the 18th century many men in England had decided that the ' new ' education could be made to pay. As a result, academies, largely of the Dotheboys Hall type, appeared in all parts of the country. These attempted to give instruction in ' science,' arithmetic, and English ; but as education was coming to be regarded as a trade rather than as an art, their work was not of a very high order. The work of the Dissenting Academies, that of keeping alive in England Realism and of breaking down the educational monopoly of the Universities and grammar schools, being accomplished, they ceased to be a definite system and became part of the main stream of education. In the meantime, the effective teaching of modern subjects and the application of the democratic principle to education awaited the social and educational awakening of the 19th century.

APPENDIX I

THE CHIEF DISSENTING ACADEMIES

This list has been compiled from information from various sources, some of which are the MS. account of Dissenting Ministers, kept at Dr Williams's Library; Calamy's *Account* and *History*; Bogue and Bennett's *History*; Toulmin's *History*; *Lives and Funeral Sermons of various ministers*; *Dictionary of National Biography*.

The academies given were Presbyterian or Independent; one, Bristol, No. 9, Period II, was Baptist, and was probably the *first* Baptist Academy—the General Baptist Education Society was not formed until 1794. The Quaker Schools, and such institutions as that started for the Methodists by George Whitefield at Kingswood 1740, are not given. The dates have been carefully examined but many of them cannot be authenticated.

ACADEMIES OF FIRST PERIOD.

1. *Broad Oak (Flint)* 1690–1706. *Tutors*, Ph. Henry, M.A. (Christ Church, Oxford). He taught Samuel Benion, who helped him with instruction of some ' young gentlemen ' (gram. school and academy). After P. Henry's death, 1696, Benion continued academical work till in 1706, after death of James Owen, he removed to Shrewsbury (see above, No. 17).

2. *Bromsgrove* (or *Stourbridge*) 1665–1692 (?). *Tutor*, Henry Hickman, B.D., Fellow of Magdalen, Oxford (d. 1692).

3. *Brynllwarch*, near *Bridgend, Glamorgan* 1668–1697 (?). *Tutor*, Samuel Jones, M.A. (Fellow and Tutor of Jesus College, Oxford). *Students*, James Owen (tutor, Shrewsbury), etc.

4. *Coventry* 1663–1700 (removed 1700 to London by Dr Oldfield). *Tutors*, Dr John Bryan (d. 1675), Dr Obadiah Grew (d. 1689), Thomas Shewell, M.A. (d. 1693), Dr Joshua Oldfield, assisted by Wm. Tong.

5. *Dartmouth* 1668–1691. *Tutor*, John Flavel, B.A. (d. 1691). *Students*, only four.

6. *Islington* (1) 1672–1680. *Tutor*, Ralph Button, M.A., B.D. (Exeter, Oxford), Fellow and Tutor of Merton (?), Oxford, 1642, Professor of Geometry in Gresham College, 1647, Canon of Christ Church and University orator (d. 1680). *Students*, Sir J. Jekyll, lawyer, etc.

7. *Islington* (2) 1672–1707 (?). Migratory (Woodford Bridge, Essex (plague), Battersea, Wimbledon, etc.). *Tutors*, Thomas Doolittle, M.A. (Pembroke, Camb.), assisted by Thomas Vincent, M.A. (Christ Church, Oxford), T. Rowe (?). *Students*, Calamy, Kerr, M.D. (tutor Highgate and Bethnal Green), Matthew Henry, etc.

8. *Knell* (*Radnorshire*) (?) 1675–(?). *Tutor*, John Weaver. *Students*, Samuel Jones, Tutor of Tewkesbury, etc.

9. *Lincoln* 1668–1680. *Tutor*, Edward Reyner, M.A. (d. 1680).

10. *Mill Hill* (?)–1701 (?). *Tutor*, Richard Swift (d. 1701).

11. *Nettlebed* (Oxon) 1666–1697. *Tutor*, Thomas Cole, M.A. (Christ Church, Oxford). John Locke was a student of Cole's before his ejectment.

12. *Newington Green* (1) 1665 (?) to about 1706. Migratory (Little Britain, Clapham). *Tutors*, Theophilus Gale, M.A., Fellow of Magdalen College, Oxford (d. 1678). T. Rowe (d. 1706). *Students*, Isaac Watts, D.D. (Edin.), Dr J. Evans, Daniel Neal, Henry Grove (Tutor at Taunton), J. Hughes (poet and dramatist), Josiah Hort (conformed—Archbishop of Tuam), etc.

13. *Newington Green* (2) 1667 (?) to about 1706. *Tutors*, Charles Morton, M.A. (Wadham College, Oxford). In 1685 he went to New England, he was succeeded by Stephen Lobb; Wm. Wickens (Emmanuel College, Cambridge), Francis Glasscock. *Students*, Daniel Defoe, Samuel Wesley, Kitt, Butterby, Wm. Jenkyn, etc.

14. *Nottingham* 1680–(?). *Tutors*, Ed. Reynolds and John Whitlock, Thos. Hardy (same academy?).

15. *Rathmell* 1669–1698. Migratory (Natland, Kendal, etc.). *Tutor*, Richard Frankland, M.A.(Christ's College, Camb.), assisted by Issot. *Students*, John Ashe, James Clegg, M.A., John Owen, T. Jollie (Tutor at Attercliffe), etc.

16. *Sheriffhales* 1663–1697 (closed before Woodhouse went to London). *Tutors*, John Woodhouse, assisted by Southwell. *Students*, Robert Harley, Henry St John, Lord Foley, Thomas Hunt, Benjamin Bennett (author of *Christian Oratory*).

17. *Shrewsbury* 1663–1730 (?). *Tutors*, Francis Tallents, M.A., Camb., Fellow, Tutor and Vice-President of Magdalen College (d. 1708), John Bryan (?) (d. 1699), James Owen (d. 1706), Samuel Benion, M.A. (d. 1708), John Reynolds (d. 1727), Dr Gyles (d. 1730 ?). *Students* (under Benion), Latham (tutor at Findern), etc.

18. *Sulby*, near *Welford, Northampton* 1680–1688. *Tutor*, John Shuttlewood, B.A. (Christ's College, Camb.).

19. *Taunton* 1672–1759 (when Amory went to London). *Tutors*, Matthew Warren, Robert Darch, Stephen James, Henry Grove, Thos. Amory, D.D. *Students*, Thomas and John Wright of Bristol, etc.

20. *Tubney* 1668–1699. *Tutor*, D. H. Langley (d. 1697).

21. *Wapping* 1675 (?) to 1680–1. *Tutor*, Ed. Veal, M.A. (Christ Church, Oxford). *Students*, Samuel Wesley, 1678–1680, etc.

22. *Whitchurch* 1668–1680 (?). *Tutor*, J. Maulden (d. 1680).

23. *Wickhambrook* 1670–1696 (?) (when tutor removed to Bishop's Stortford). *Tutor*, Samuel Cradock, B.D. (Emmanuel College, Camb.). *Students*, Edmund Calamy, D.D., etc.

ACADEMIES OF SECOND PERIOD.

1. *Attercliffe* 1691–1744. *Tutors*, Timothy Jollie (d. 1714), John De la Rose, J. Wadsworth (?). *Students*, Nicholas Saunderson, J. Bowles (Lord Chancellor of Ireland), Jennings of Kibworth Academy, Samuel Price, Thomas Bradbury, etc.

2. *Alcester* (?)–1720 (?). Joseph Porter, on whose death students were removed to Stratford-on-Avon (see below, No. 29).

3. *Abergavenny* 1757–(?). Fund Board withdrew their support from the Carmarthen Academy and established one of their own. Migratory (Oswestry, Wrexham, Llanfyllin, Newton), *Brecon College since* 1839. *Tutors*, David Jardine (d. 1766), Benj. Davis, D.D. (d. 1787), Ed. Williams, Jenkin Lewis, George Lewis, D.D. (d. 1822), etc.

4. *Bedworth* 1690–(?). *Tutors*, Julius Saunders and John Kirkpatrick.

5. *Bethnal Green* 1680(?)–1696(?). Migratory (Highgate, Clerkenwell). *Tutors*, John Kerr, M.D. *Students*, Samuel Palmer, etc.

6. *Bridgenorth* 1726–1740 (?). *Tutor*, Fleming, who removed to Stratford-on-Avon (No. 29) when John Alexander went to Dublin.

7. *Bridgewater* (?)–1747. *Tutor*, John Moore, M.A. (d. 1747).

8. *Bolton* 1723–1729. *Tutor*, John Barclay, M.A.

9. *Bristol* 1720–(?). First Baptist Academy. *Tutor*, Foskett, continued the work of Ed. Terril and Caleb Tope.

10. *Carmarthen* 1700–present day. Migratory (Llwynllwyd, Haverford West, etc., Carmarthen, and probably continuation of Brynllwarch : see No. 3, Period I). *Tutors*, Wm. Evans, Thos. Perrot (under whom were about 150 pupils) (d. 1733 or 1734), Vavasor Griffiths, Evans Davis, etc.

11. *Exeter* (about) 1700–1722. *Tutor*, Joseph Hallet. Academy declined and was closed because of a subscription quarrel.

12. *Findern* (?)–1754, afterwards at Derby. *Tutors*, Thomas Hill (d. 1720), Samuel Latham, M.D. (d. 1754).

13. *Gosport* 1789–(?). *Tutor*, David Bogue, M.A. 1800 the Missionary Society placed their missionaries under Bogue for preparation.

14. *Gloucester* 1696–(?). *Tutor*, James Forbes (d. 1712).

15. *Hungerford* 1696–1701(?). *Tutor*, Benjamin Robinson, educated at Sheriffhales (d. 1722 or 1724).

16. *Hoxton Square* 1700–1729 (?), removed to Hoxton Square from Coventry (see No. 4, Period I). *Tutors*, Joshua Oldfield, D.D., John Spodeman, M.A., Lorimer, M. Capel.

17. *Heckmondwyke* 1756, merged in Rotherham College. *Tutors*, James Scott (d. 1783), Samuel Walker, etc.

18. *Idle* 1800, merged in Airedale. *Tutor*, Wm. Vint. 1886 Rotherham and Airedale became Yorkshire United College, Bradford.

19. *Ipswich* 1698–1734(?). *Tutor*, John Langton (d. 1704).

20. *Kendal* 1733–1752. *Tutor*, Dr Caleb Rotherham.

21. *Lyme Regis* or *Colyton* 1690, removed to Shepton Mallet and then to Poole. *Tutors*, John Short, Matthew Towgood.

22. *London* (various parts) 1696–1744 supported by Fund Board. Migratory (Pinner, Moorfields: see Newington Green, No. 24, Period II). *Tutors*, Thos. Goodwin, Isaac Chauncey, M.A., M.D., Thos. Ridgley, D.D., John Eames, F.R.S., Jos. Densham.

23. *Manchester* 1698–1710 (?), countenanced by and promised support from the Lancashire ministers. *Tutors*, John Chorlton (d. 1705), John Conningham, M.A. *Students*, J. Clegg, etc.

24. *Newington Green* 1730–1744–1850, established by King's Head Society. Migratory (Deptford, Stepney, Addle Street (whither it removed in 1744 after having joined the Fund Board Academy [No. 22, Period II]), Mile End, Homerton), now represented by New College, London. *Tutors*, Abraham Taylor, D.D., Samuel Parsons, John Hubbard after 1744, Zephaniah Marryat, D.D., John Conder, D.D., etc. (see Northampton, No. 26, Period II).

25. *Newport Pagnell* 1783, merged in Cheshunt (?). *Tutors*, W. Bull, J. Bull, M.A., J. Watson, W. Foggart.

26. *Northampton* 1715 (?), represented by New College, London. Migratory (started at Kibworth under John Jennings, moved to Hinkley, Harborough, and in 1729 to Northampton. After 1752 to Daventry, back to Northampton, Wymondley, Byng Place, and 1850 merged in New College, London). *Tutors*, John Jennings

(d. 1723), Philip Doddridge, D.D., Caleb Ashworth, Thos. Robins, Thos. Belsham, John Horsey, Wm. Parry, etc.

27. *Ottery St Mary* 1752–(?), started by Congregational Fund Board, now represented by Bristol. Migratory (Bridport, Taunton, Exeter, Plymouth, Bristol). *Tutors*, J. Lavington, James Rooker, Thomas Reader, James Small, etc.

28. *Saffron Walden* 1680–(?). *Tutor*, John Payne, assisted by Fund Board when the latter was first started.

29. *Stratford-on-Avon* 1715 (?) at Gloucester. (?) *Tutors*, John Alexander, who 1729 went to Dublin; John Fleming, who had begun an academy at Bridgenorth (1726–1727), then went to Stratford.

30. *Tiverton* (?)–(?). *Tutor*, John Moor (d. 1740).

31. *Tewkesbury* 1680 (Gloucester) to 1719, moved to Tewkesbury in 1712. *Tutor*, S. Jones (d. 1719 or 1720). *Students*, Secker, Chandler, Butler, etc.

32. *Warrington* 1700–1746. *Tutor*, Charles Owen, D.D. (d. 1746).

33. *Wellclose Square* 1744–1785, removed to Hoxton in 1762. *Tutors*, Samuel M. Savage, D.D., David Jennings, D.D., Andrew Kippis, D.D., Abraham Rees, D.D., F.R.S.

34. *Whitehaven* 1710–1723. *Tutor*, Thos. Dixon, M.A., M.D. *Students*, John Taylor (at Warrington, No. 3, Period III), Geo. Benson, Caleb Rotherham. Removed to Bolton 1723–1729 (?). (See No. 8, Period II.)

ACADEMIES OF THIRD PERIOD.

1. *Exeter* 1760–1786. *Tutors*, Samuel Merivale, Michah Towgood, John Turner, John Hogg, Thos. Jervis. *Students* (see Appendix No. V).

2. *London* 1760–(?). *Tutor*, Samuel Pike, 'a less literary seminary but it continued only for a few years.'

3. *Warrington* 1757–1783. Library moved to Manchester New College, 1783; other removals, York (1803), Manchester, London, now represented by Manchester College,

Oxford. *Tutors*, Dr Taylor, Dr Aikin, J. Holt, J. Priestley, LL.D., Wm. Enfield, etc.; at Manchester, Thos. Barnes, D.D., George Walker, F.R.S., John Dalton, D.C.L., LL.D., F.R.S., Ralph Harrison, etc.; and at York, Charles Wellbeloved, Hugh Kerr, M.A., etc. *Students* (see Appendix No. V).

APPENDIX II

COURSE AT KIBWORTH UNDER REV. JOHN JENNINGS

Source. Letter from Ph. Doddridge (student) to Rev. Saunders, 1728: 'Our course of Education at Kibworth was the employment of four years and every half year we entered upon a new set of studies or at least changed the time and order of our lectures.'

Year	Subject	Lectures per week	Notes on Books and Method
1st half-year	Geometry or Algebra	3	Barrow's Euclid Book 1 and then started (a) fundamental operations, Algebra and arithmetic; (b) reduction of equations. } System drawn up by Jennings.
			'Under every head we had demonstration as well as practical rules.'
	Hebrew	2	Bythner's Grammar.
	Geography	1	Gordon's Geog. 'Lecture only an examination of the account which we could give of the most remarkable passages.'
	French	1	Boyer's Grammar. } 'Without regarding pronunciation with which Mr Jennings was not acquainted.' Familiar phrases and dialogues. }
	Latin	1 (1 hr.)	Selections from Suetonius, Tacitus, Seneca, etc., and especially Cicero. *Method.* 1st to read Latin according to grammatical order of the words and then render it into as elegant English as we could.

Year	Subject	Lectures per week	Notes on Books and Method
1st half-year	Classical Exercises	1 (1 hr.)	Latin-English, English-Latin, many passages in Spectator and Tatler, both serious and humorous.
2nd half-year	Geometry and Algebra	2	Euclid Books III, IV, and VI.
	Logic	2	Burgesdicius in about six lectures. Mr Jenning's system, 'a great deal of which was taken from Mr Locke.'
	Civil History	2	Puffendorf's Intro. to Hist. of Europe with Crull's continuation and his History of Asia, Africa and America. History of England. Dupin's Compendium. Spanheim's Elenchus. King's Constitution, etc. — 'We read these just as we did Gordon,' *i.e.* in private, and were questioned at the lecture.
	French	2	Telemachus. Selections from Bourdeleau's sermons. 'Perhaps, if we had tasted a greater variety of authors it had better answered our end.'
	Latin Poets and exercises	1	Virgil, Horace, Terence, Lucretius, Juvenal, Plautus, etc.
	Hebrew	1	
	Oratory and exercises of reading and delivery	1	Oratory exercises. 'Bacon's Essays often used, and our exercises were a kind of comment upon some remarkable sentences they contained.'
3rd half-year	Mechanics	2	System on lever, screw, pulley, wedge, etc.
	Hydro-statics	2	Abridgment of some of Mr Eames's lectures.
	Physics	2	Le Clerc's system.
	Greek Poets	1	Theocritus, Homer, Pindar, 'I do not remember that we ever read in our public course any Greek History, oratory or philosophy.'

Year	Subject	Lectures per week	Notes on Books and Method
3rd half-year	History of England	1	Browne's 2 vols., 'which in the main were very good.'
	Anatomy	1	Eames's in English. 'We took in the collateral assistance of Nievwentyt, Keil and Cheselden.'
	Use of Globes	1	Jones.
	Astronomy	1 ⎫	Mr Jennings' system printed amongst
	Chronology	1 ⎬	his Miscellanies.
	Miscellanies	1	Short sketches of Fortification, Heraldry, Architecture, Psalmody, Physiognomy, Metaphysics, etc.
	Logical Disputations	1	{ Disputations in English. / Thesis in Latin. } Neither in a syllogistic form.
			'One of the class made the thesis, each of the rest read an exercise either in prose or verse, English or Latin. I think English orations were the most common and turned, I believe, to the best account.'
4th half-year	Pneumatology	2	Mr Jennings. 'This with our divinity, which was a continuation of it, was by far the most valuable part of our course. Mr Jennings had bestowed a vast deal of thought upon them and his discourses from them in the lecture room were admirable.'
	Physics	1	
	Miscellanies	1	
	Jewish Antiquities	2	Abridgment of Mr Jones's (Tewkesbury) notes on Godwin with some very curious and important additions.
5th half-year	Ethics	2	Grotius. Puffendorf. Wollaston's Religion of Nature Delineated.
	Critics	1	Abridgment of Mr Jones's.
	Pneumatologised disputation	1	

Year	Subject	Lectures per week	Notes on Books and Method
6th half-year	Divinity	3	
	Christian Antiquities	1	Sir Peter King's Constitution of the Primitive Church with The Original Draught in answer to it.
	Miscellanies	1	
	Homily	1	' Of a Thursday night.'
7th half-year	Divinity	3	
	Ecclesiastical History	1	Dupin's Compendium—' very defective in places.'
	Sermon	1	' On art of preaching and pastoral care Mr Jennings gave us very excellent advice, and some valuable hints on the head of Nonconformity.'
	Theological Disputation	1	
8th half-year	Divinity	1	
	History of Controversies	1	Spanheim's Elenchus.
	Miscellanies	1	Vol. II—a brief historical account of ancient philosophy.
	Theological Disputation	1	' We preached this last half year, either at home or abroad as occasion required and towards the beginning of it were examined by a committee of neighbouring ministers to whom that office was assigned at a preceding general meeting.'

APPENDIX III

DISCIPLINE IN DISSENTING ACADEMIES

Rules of Doddridge's Academy.

Source. A History of Castle Hill Church, Northampton, contains a copy of the original manuscript book now at New College, London.

Extracts from the rules are given below.

Constitution, Orders and Rules relating to the Academy at Northampton agreed upon by the Tutors and the several members of it in December 1740 and then established as the future conditions of Admission into the Academy or continuance in it.

SECTION I. OF ACADEMICAL STUDIES.

1. *1st year.* Translations from Latin into English and vice versa as appointed by the Tutors to be showed them at the day and hour appointed and in the last three months of the year orations are to be exhibited in Latin and English alternately every Thursday which is also to be the time of the following exercises.

2. In first half of second year these orations are to be continued and in the latter part of the year each is in his turn to exhibit a Philosophical Thesis or Dissertation.

3. In third year Ethical Theses or Dissertations are to be exhibited weekly as above and toward the end of this year and during the fourth, Theological.

4. The Revolution of these is to be so adjusted that every student may compose at least six orations, Theses or Dissertations before the conclusion of his fourth year.

5. All subjects to be disputed upon are to be given out with the names of the Respondent and opponent—at least as soon as the Academy meets after the long vacation and at Christmas and, if possible, before the vacation.

6. The absence of the Tutor is not to occasion the omission of any of these exercises...etc.

7. Exercises are to be first written in a paper book, then reviewed and corrected by one of the Tutors, after that, fairly transcribed and after they have been exhibited in the manner which shall be appointed, a fair copy of them, with the author's name annexed, shall be delivered to the Tutor.

8. Two sermons on given subjects to be composed by every theological student in his eighth half year to be read over by him in the class and having been there corrected to be preached in the family if the student does not propose preaching in public before he leave the Academy, and besides these, at least six schemes of other sermons on given texts are to be exhibited in the class during the fourth year by each student.

9. If any student continue a fifth year he is to compose at least one sermon and exhibit two schemes every quarter whether he do or do not preach in public. Besides which he is this fifth year to exhibit and defend two large Theological theses....

10. Four classics viz.: one Greek and one Latin poet and one Greek and one Latin prose writer as appointed by the Tutor are to be read by each student in his study and observations are to be written upon them to be kept in a distinct book, and communicated to the Tutor whenever he shall think fit.

11. Each student of the upper class may be allowed to propose a difficult scripture to the Principal Tutor every Thursday to be discussed by him the next Thursday. But it will be expected that the person proposing them write some memorandum of the solution...etc.

12. ...each Theological Pupil will be expected to write, either at meeting or afterward....Hints of all the Sermons he hears, to be examined by the Tutor...etc.

13. On the four Thursdays preceding the long vacation, the whole Academy is to meet at ten in the morning and all the forenoon is to be spent in the examination of Students.... And on the first of these days Disputations shall be held by the two upper classes in the Presence of the Juniors that they may learn by example the method of Disputation...etc.

14. In case of a total neglect of preparing an appointed exercise sixpence is to be forfeited to the box....

Section II. Of Attendance on Family Prayer and Lecture at Appointed Times.

1.   Every Student boarding in the House is to be present at the calling over the names in the great parlour at 10 minutes after six in the morning or to forfeit a penny.

2.   Family Prayer is to begin in the morning at eight o'clock and in the evening at seven...and every one absenting himself from either...is to forfeit two pence.

3.   Every student is to be ready for Lecture...within five minutes of the Hour fixed for the beginning...or to forfeit two pence, and if Lecture be entirely neglected and no reason can be assigned which the Tutor (who is always to be the judge of such reasons) shall think sufficient, he is to be publicly reproved at the next meeting of the whole Society, and if the neglect be repeated within a month he is to have some extraordinary exercise appointed as the Tutor shall think fit.

4.   Each Pupil, after he hath entered on the second half year of his course, shall take his turn at family prayer in the evening...etc.

5.   ...nor shall a change of turns be permitted without the Tutor's express leave.

6.   If the person whose turn it is to go to Prayer in the evening absent himself and have not procured another to officiate for him he shall forfeit sixpence or take his turn twice together...etc.

Section III. Of the Hours, Place and Order of Meals.

1.   The time of breakfast is to be from the end of family prayer till 5 minutes before Ten.

2.   It is to be eaten either in the Hall or the great parlour, a blessing having first been asked by the senior Pupil present at each table if the Assistant Tutor be not at one of them.

3.   They that choose tea in the morning may either breakfast with the Tutor in his parlour, or at the other tea board in the great parlour, each, in that case, providing his own tea and sugar in a just proportion as the company shall agree.

4.   Dinner is to be set on the table precisely at two when every student is to be in the Hall before the blessing...and not to leave the room till thanks be returned.

5.   Supper is to be eaten in the Hall between the conclusion of evening prayer and 9 o'clock...etc.

6.   Neither breakfast, dinner nor supper is to be carried into any room, besides that appointed for the family meal, except in case of sickness...etc.

7.   As making toasts and butter and toasting cheese has been found to be more expensive than can conveniently be afforded on the usual terms here, that custom is to be disused except by the Parlour boarders.

9.   ......
10.   ......

Section IV.   Of shutting up the Gate and retiring to Bed.

1.   The gate is to be locked every night at ten and the key is to be brought to the Tutor or his Assistant and every Pupil who comes in after that time is to forfeit two pence for every quarter of an hour that he hath exceeded ten.

2.   If any one go out of the house without express permission, after the gate is locked, he is to pay One shilling for such offence and should any one get into the house irregularly after the door is locked he and each person assisting him in such irregular entry must expect that immediate information will be sent to his friends.

3.   If any pupil procure a key for the gate he shall not only forfeit it as soon as discovered but be fined two shillings and sixpence.

4.   If any one keep a guest beyond half an hour past ten he shall forfeit for every quarter of an hour which such guest stays as if he had stayed abroad himself.

5.   If any one stay out all night and do not the next day of his own accord take an opportunity of acquainting the Tutor or assistant with it and giving reason for so extraordinary a conduct, he must expect that if it afterward come to the Tutor's knowledge an immediate complaint will be

lodged with his friends without any previous notice taken of it to him.

6. An Account is to be brought to the Tutor every Saturday morning by the person who has kept the key the preceding week, of every one who has been let in during that time after ten o'clock.

Section V. Rules relating to the Chambers and Closets.

1. That the Chambers and Closets be chosen by persons paying the same price according to the seniority of classes... etc.

2. ......

3. ......

4. That if Windows be broke, furniture wantonly demolished or any other hurt be done to the House by the fault of any of the pupils the repair...be charged to the person by whom it is done. N.B. This extends to the instruments of the apparatus and even to any detriment which may arise to them by the carelessness...etc.

5. ......

6. ......

Section VI. Rules relating to the Library.

1. Every pupil is to pay a guinea to the Library when he enters on the second year of his course if he propose to go through the whole ; but if he purpose to stay only two years he is to pay but half a guinea and that from the time he enters on the second half year.

2–10. Ordinary rules for borrowing and returning books.

Section VII. Rules relating to the Office of the Monitor.

1. Every Academical student in the Family is to be monitor in his turn excepting only the Senior Class for the time being, and if any of them shall, in his turn, choose to officiate as monitor his assistance shall be thankfully accepted.

2. The monitor is to call up every student at six o'clock in the morning, winter and summer, Vacation times only excepted, and having rung the bell twice at ten minutes after six is to call over all the names, distinguishing on his bill those who are absent and for every quarter of an hour for which he delays he is to forfeit two pence. He is also to call over his list before morning and evening prayer as above, as also before all Lectures appointed for the whole Academy, together, and if he fail to do it...he is to forfeit sixpence for every such failure.

3. He is to review the Library on Saturday at 3 in the afternoon and to call over the catalogue of the books wanting, according to Section VI. No. 7, under a forfeiture of a shilling and he is to see that a pen and ink be left in the Library for public use.

4. He is to lay up the Bibles and Psalm books after prayer in the cupboard...and as an acknowledgment for that trouble is to claim one farthing for every one who shall neglect to bring his Psalm book with him at those times, if he choose generally to keep it in his closet.

5. The monitor is to have an eye on the door to see whether any one goes out during divine service and to inform the Tutor of it and is to send the junior pupil present to call the Tutor if in the House as soon as he begins to call over the names.

Section VIII. Rules relating to Conduct Abroad.

1. No student is to go into a Publick House to drink there on penalty of a public censure for the first time and the forfeiture of a shilling the second; unless some particular occasion arise which shall, in the judgment of the Tutor, be deemed a sufficient reason.

2. No one is to begin a P.M. at any place in the town without the knowledge and approbation of the Tutor.

3. If any one spread reports abroad to the dishonour of the family or any member of it he must expect a public reproof and to hear a caution given to others to beware of placing any confidence in him.

Section IX. Miscellaneous Rules not comprehended under the former sections.

3.   When the small pecuniary fines here appointed evidently appear to be despised, they will be exchanged for some extraordinary exercises, which, if they are not performed, must occasion complaint to the Friends of the student in question ; for the intent of these laws is not to enrich the box at the expense of those who are determined to continue irregular but to prevent any from being so.

5.   Accounts with the Tutor are to be balanced twice a year and all bills from tradesmen, if such there be, are to be delivered in to the Tutor by the persons from whom they are due, at the seasons at which they respectively know their accounts are to be made up.

6.   No student is to board abroad unless at the desire and under the direction of the tutor.   And those who do so board abroad are, nevertheless, to attend family prayers and lectures at the appointed times.

7.   The news bought for the use of the family is to be paid for out of the box.

8.   ......

9.   In the absence of the Principal Tutor the Assistant Tutor is to be regarded as his deputy...etc.

10.   ...If any gentlemen, not intended for the ministry ...take up their abode amongst us, whatever their rank in life be, it is expected and insisted upon that they govern themselves by these rules, excepting those which directly relate to exercises preparatory to the ministry...etc.

P. Doddridge, D.D.   *Dec.* 10*th*, 1743.
T. Brabant.

We whose names are hereunto subscribed do hereby declare our Acquiescence in these Constitutions, Orders and Rules as the terms of our respective Admission into or continuance in the Academy at Northampton.

Then follow 63 signatures.

APPENDIX IV

WARRINGTON (PERIOD III) LIBRARY

Source. ' Select Catalogue of Books in the Library belonging to the Warrington Academy,' printed by Eyres for the academy in 1775.

The catalogue is arranged under subjects as follows :

1. Greek and Roman Classics, 70 titles (separate volumes not counted).
2. Translations, 19.
3. Dictionaries, Grammars (Latin, Greek, Hebrew, French, Italian), 36—among which are Priestley's *Grammar*, Seddon's *Lectures on Grammar*, Ward's *Essays on the English Language*.
4. Biography, 50. The following, chosen at random, exhibit a catholic taste : *Lives of the Professors of Gresham College—Lives of the Philosophers*, Voltaire's *Charles XII*, *Cromwell*, *Pope Sextus V*, *Mahomet*, *Ignatius*, *Sully*, *Descartes*, *Memoires de Philippe de Commines.*
5. History, Chronology, Geography, Voyages, Travels, 82. This list is interesting as showing what means the students had of reading in these modern subjects and is therefore given in full (see next page).
6. Mathematics, Natural Philosophy, etc., 81.
7. Politics, Commerce and Law, 40.
8. Sermons, 41.
9. Morals and Metaphysics, 25.
10. Evidences of Christianity and Ecclesiastical History, 67.
11. Theological and Scripture Criticism, 85.
12. Miscellanies, 78 (given in full).

*Complete List of Books in Section 5—History,
Geography, etc.*

Kircheri's Chinae Historia.

Purchas's Pilgrim, 5 vols.

Prideaux's Introduction to History.

History of the Reign of Queen Elizabeth.

Thuani Historia, 4 vols.

Macaulay's History of England, 4 vols.

Hume's History of England, 8 vols.

Vertot's Roman Revolution, 2 vols.

Fresnoy on History, 2 vols.

Ludlow's Memories, 3 vols.

Buonamici's Commentaries on the Wars of Italy.

Swift's Memoirs of the four last years of Queen Anne.

Strauchius's Chronology.

Holberg's Introduction to Universal History, by Sharp.

Methodus Legendi Historiae, A. Wheer.

Philips's Account of Malabar.

Bernier's History of the Empire of the Great Mogul.

Mainbourgh's Histoire de la Décadence de l'Empire après
    Charlemagne.

Fontenelle's History of Sweden.

Spon's History of Germany.

Nicholson's English Historical Library.

Ricaut's History of Peru.

Le Bruyn's Travels.

Raleigh's History of the World.

Newton's Chronology.

Hooke's Roman History, 4 vols.

Buchanani opera, 2 vols.

Robertson's History of Scotland, 2 vols.

    —— History of Charles II, 3 vols.

Bacon's History of Henry VII.

Rapin's History of England, 21 vols.

La Motte's Animadversion upon ancient Historians.

Puffendorf's History of Sweden.

    —— Introduction to History, 3 vols.

De Wit's Republic of Holland.
Savage's History of Germany.
Sprat's History of the Royal Society.
Bolingbroke on the Study of History.
Temple's Works.
Pitt's History of the Mahometans.
Montesquieu's Reflections on Rome.
Josephus's Works, 6 vols.
Memoirs of the House of Brandenburg.
Malley's Observations on the Romans.
Gleidanus de quatuor Imperiis.
Magna Charta.
Davies's Introduction for History.
Martinii Historia.
Harris's Voyages and Travels, 2 vols.
Blair's Chronology.
Antient and Modern Universal History, 65 vols.
Goldsmith's History of England, 4 vols.
Kennet's Roman Antiquities.
Potter's Antiquities of Greece.
Verenius's Geography, 2 vols.
Lockman's Jesuit, travels, 2 vols.
Memoirs of Pollnitz, 4 vols.
Geographia Classica.
Gage's Survey of the West Indies.
Burnet's Travels through Italy and Switzerland.
Warwick's Memoirs of Charles II.
History of the East Indies.
Ray's Travels through the Low Countries, 2 vols.
Jennings on the Use of Globes.
Bacon's History of England.
Stowe's Survey of London.
History of Switzerland.
History of Denmark.
History of Sweden.
Reign of James I, by Overbury.
Rollin's Antient History, 10 vols.
Letters on History of English, 2 vols.

Pomponius Mela de Situ Orbis.
Reign of Richard II.
Hayward's Reign of Edward VI.
Ray's Journey through Germany, Italy and France.
Les Voyages de Tavernier, 2 vols.
Campbell's Present State of Europe.
La Houtan's Voyages to North America, 2 vols.
Herrira's History of America, 6 vols.
Marigny's History of the Arabians, 4 vols.
Lyttelton's Life of Henry II, 6 vols.

Miscellanies.

Gil Blas, 4 vols.
Shakespeare's Works, 9 vols.
Tales of a Tub.
Osborne's Works.
Bacon's Remains.
Batteaux's Principes de la Littérature, 5 vols.
Oeuvres de Rapin, 3 vols.
Oeuvres de Fontenelle, 2 vols.
Oeuvres de Boileau, 3 vols.
Clerici ars critica.
Dodsley's Poems, 6 vols.
Gray's Poems.
Prior's Poems, 2 vols.
Milton's Paradise Lost and Paradise Regained, 2 vols.
Pope's Works, 6 vols.
Thomson's Works, 4 vols.
Baker's Medalla Portarum Romanorum, 2 vols.
Akenside's Pleasures of the Imagination.
Boileau's Works, 2 vols.
Young's Night Thoughts.
Hudibras.
Bruyère's Works, 2 vols.
Letters concerning Mythology.
Ray's English Proverbs.
Chaucer's Tales.
Hughes's Miscellany.

Dryden's Fables.
Occasional Papers, 2 vols.
Shaftesbury's Characteristics.
Fontenelle's Dialogues of the Dead.
Reflections on Poetry and Painting.
Kain's Elements of Criticism, 3 vols.
Fordyce's Dialogues on Education.
Mrs Montague's Remarks on the Writings and Genius of
    Shakespeare.
Rapin's Critical Works, 2 vols.
Young's Love of Fame.
Hogarth's Analysis of Beauty.
Middleton's Works, 4 vols.
Sheridan on Elocution.
Hill's Review of the Royal Society.
Boffu on Epic Poetry.
Lettres du Voiture.
Waller's Poems.
Instructive Histories, 2 vols.
Spence on Pope's Odyssey.
Cato's Letters, 4 vols.
Erasmus's Apothegms of the Antients, 2 vols.
Independent Whig, 4 vols.
The Guardian, 2 vols.
Addison's Miscellanies, 4 vols.
Freeholder.
Private Life of the Romans.
Goldsmith's Essays.
Hurd's Commentaries on Horace, 3 vols.
Webb on Poetry.
Gerard on Taste.
Spectator, 8 vols.
World, 4 vols.
Philips's Poems.
Mason's Poems.
Wharton's Essay on the Writings and Genius of Pope.
Fitzosborne's Letters.
Burke on Sublime and Beautiful.

Lyttelton's Dialogues of the Dead.
Harris's Treatises on Art, Music, Painting and Poetry, Happiness.
Rice on Reading.
Letters concerning Taste.
Ward's Oratory, 2 vols.
Swift's Miscellany, 2 vols.
Congreve's Works, 2 vols.
Cambray on Eloquence
Nourfe's Essays.
Locke's Familiar Letters.
Halifax's Works.
Cousinus de Eloquentia.
Peddon's Lectures on Oratory, MS., 2 vols.
Blount's Remarks on Poetry.
Cowley's Works.

APPENDIX V

STUDENTS AT WARRINGTON (PERIOD III)

Source. List of Students in *Monthly Repository*, Vol. IX. *Total Number*, 1757–1782, is 393 (see table p. 160).

Entered for Law	..	.. ..	22
,, ,, Medicine		.. ..	24
,, ,, Divinity		.. ..	52
,, ,, Commerce		.. ..	98
Course not specified ..		.. ..	197

' Commerce ' seems to indicate merchants, bankers, etc. ; brewers, shopkeepers—all ' tradesmen ' are among the ' unspecified' and also many who entered the army and some who were ' country gentlemen.' These had a good ' general ' education.

STUDENTS AT EXETER (1760 PERIOD III)

Source. MS. in Dr Williams's Library.

Total Number on list is 93. Among those whose calling is given are

- 6 attorneys or barristers.
- 4 ministers[1].
- 7 physicians.
- 24 merchants or ' trade.'
- 7 navy or navy office men.
- 13 esquires.
- 2 apothecaries.
- 3 army men.

Table showing number of students entered for various causes in different years at Warrington, 1757–1782.

Year	Medicine	Law	Divinity	Commerce	Unspecified	Total
1757	1	—	1	3	—	5
1758	3	—	3	6	6	18
1759	1	1	5	2	7	16
1760	1	—	2	5	4	12
1761	1	3	2	7	4	17
1762	—	—	4	4	1	9
1763	2	—	1	4	4	11
1764	1	—	—	12	5	18
1765	2	—	1	11	8	22
1766	—	—	1	5	9	15
1767	—	—	1	—	8	9
1768	—	1	2	5	8	16
1769	—	2	3	6	7	18
1770	1	—	2	—	5	8
1771	—	2	—	5	13	20
1772	2	1	1	3	16	23
1773	1	—	2	1	3	7
1774	—	2	3	2	5	12
1775 / 1776	2	4	3	3	11	23
1777	3	—	6	3	11	23
1778	—	3	2	9	13	27
1779	—	3	1	1	18	23
1780	—	1	3	1	14	19
1781	1	1	3	—	9	14
1782	—	—	—	—	8	8
	22	24	52	98	197	393

[1] A list in the *Monthly Repository*, Vol. XIII. is different ; 12 ministers are mentioned and only 49 names are given.

APPENDIX VI

PRIESTLEY'S SUGGESTIONS FOR STUDY OF HISTORY
AND GEOGRAPHY

Source. Miscellaneous works containing Essay on Education and Syllabuses of lectures in History given at Warrington.
The following extracts from Priestley's syllabuses show his treatment of History in his lectures.

SYLLABUS OF COURSE OF LECTURES ON THE
STUDY OF HISTORY.

I. *General Uses of history.*
II. *Sources of history* in oral traditions, poems, monuments, coins, Heraldry, use of archives, books not properly history, language.
III. *What is necessary or useful to be known previous to the Study of History*—philosophical knowledge in general, Geography, Chronology, methods of the estimation of riches and power of ancient nations—money values etc.
IV. *Directions for facilitating the study of history*—Compendiums, Chronology, tables, Sturt's tables, Chart, History of biography, Fortifications explained—model cut in wood.
V. *Order in which histories may be read and method of studying English History*—Gildas, Bede, Geoffrey of Monmouth, Matthew Paris, R. Higden, Froissart, Thomas of Walsingham, William Caxton, John Ross, Robert Fabian...Hollingshead...Clarendon, Whitlock and Ludlow, Burnet, Rapin, Hume, Robertson, Histories of particular lives and reigns—of William the Conqueror, by William of Poictiers; Edward II, by Thomas de la More; Henry V, by Titus Livius;

Edward IV, by Haddington; Edward V, by Sir Thomas More; Henry VII, by Sir Francis Bacon; Henry VIII, by Lord Herbert of Cherbury; Edward VI's own diary; Elizabeth, by Camden. Lives written by Harris and others, Ecclesiastical writers, Burnet's History of the Reformation, Cranmer's Memorials, Littleton and Coke; Year Books; Reports; records; proclamations.

VI. *The most important objects of attention to a Reader of History*—Biography—cause and effect should be noted in all changes of human affairs. Ancient and European History; English History; most interesting periods in the history of Literature and Arts from earliest antiquity to the present time; History of Commerce; government despotism; advantages of democracy. English government traced from the constitution of the ancient German States.... How feuds became hereditary... how the clergy became an essential part of the state... method of administering justice.... Feudal system.... Rise of Corporations.... Decline of Feudalism not equal in all parts.... Expenses of government... necessity of attention to agriculture... fisheries... balance of trade—interfering of the legislature in commerce— Navigation Acts; use of colonies; uniformity of weights and measures; dreadful consequence of a total depravity of manners; Gaming; Education; food; dress and habitation; ramparts; methods of fighting, etc.

'Together with the study of history, I would advise that more attention be given to Geography than I believe is generally given to it; particularly to ...commercial geography, exhibiting the state of the world with respect to commerce, pointing out the most advantageous situations for carrying it on; and more especially noting those articles in the Natural History of countries which are, or may be, the proper subjects of commerce. This branch of

knowledge is as yet very much confined. We are probably strangers to some of the most useful productions of the earth on which we live, but a general attention once excited to the subject by teaching it to youth in all places of liberal education would be the best provision for extending it......a knowledge of chemistry is absolutely necessary to the extension of this useful branch of science (commercial geography).'

INDEX